Bar Harbor's Gilded Century
Opulence to Ashes, 1850–1950

Lydia Bodman Vandenbergh

Edited by

Earle G. Shettleworth, Jr.

Down East

Text copyright © 2009 by Lydia Bodman Vandenbergh and Earle G. Shettleworth, Jr.

ISBN (13-digit): 978-0-89272-705-6

Library of Congress Cataloging-in-Publication Data

Vandenbergh, Lydia Bodman.

Bar Harbor's gilded century : opulence to ashes / by Lydia B. Vandenbergh ; edited by

Earle G. Shettleworth, Jr.

p. cm.

Includes bibliographical references.

ISBN 978-0-89272-705-6 (trade pbk. : alk. paper)

1. Bar Harbor (Me.)--History--19th century. 2. Bar Harbor (Me.)--History--20th

century. 3. Bar Harbor (Me.)--Pictorial works. I. Shettleworth, Earle G. II. Title.

F29.B3V36 2009

974.1'45--dc22

2009005712

Design by Rich Eastman

Printed at Versa Press

5   4   3   2   1

Down East
BOOKS·MAGAZINE·ONLINE
www.downeast.com

Distributed to the trade by National Book Network

To my husband, David, who for almost twenty-five years has supported me in these Maine projects. —LBV

THANK HEAVENS for Victorians with cameras and the naturalists who preserved the beauty of Mount Desert Island. Without their efforts, we would not have been able to share this story.

Photo courtesy of the Bar Harbor Historical Society

Contents

Introduction: A Century of Change

When my daughter Christina, at age five, looked at a photograph of her great-grandmother at the same age bathing in an antique tub and asked, "But where are the faucets?" I realized the power of photographs to tell stories of the past. With the help of Earle Shettleworth, an architectural historian, I have assembled a collection of photographs that tell the story of how Bar Harbor (earlier called Eden) changed over a century.

There are many illustrated books on Bar Harbor, and most focus on one subject, such as the grandiose cottages or the Native Americans. With this volume, I've attempted to show a broader perspective of the town and the changes that occurred there from just before the Civil War to the post World War II years. Some of the changes experienced by the islanders during that century parallel those of the elite summer visitors, though on a different scale. Unlike other works, this book combines some familiar photos with many that have never been published, such as the portrait of Alpheus Hardy, the first cottager in Bar Harbor. When paired with the islanders' own voices, from diaries and interviews, these historic images convey a sense of the people and their experiences.

Bar Harbor began this century-long span as a typical nineteenth-century rural Maine community of residents who lived off the land and sea. Unlike most other villages, however, Bar Harbor offered a unique diversity of pristine beauty on a single island. The mountains, woodlands, sea cliffs, and ocean attracted artists such as Thomas Cole, who filled canvases with images of the island's beauty. These paintings, along with newspaper and magazine articles, advertised Mount Desert Island to the growing middle class, who were becoming increasingly interested—and able—to take vacations to escape the overcrowded and polluted cities. Each year after the Civil War, the number of visitors to Bar Harbor increased. These first "rusticators," as they were called, were initially housed in the homes of local residents. Some of these hosts saw an opportunity for greater profit and soon turned their carpentry skills from boats to hotels, launching what would come to be called Bar Harbor's Hotel Era.

The images on the following pages show the progression from modest to elaborate hotels, followed by a similar pattern for "cottages" as wealthy rusticators chose to build their own summer homes rather than staying in hotels. The earliest cottages were designed to blend in with the woodland setting and rocky coast, but as the area became the playground for America's aristocracy, newer summer residents built palaces

Photo courtesy of the Maine Historic Preservation Commission

to stand out and draw attention in a competition for recognition and prestige. With the rise of the Cottage Era came a surge of exclusive organizations, such as the Kebo Valley Club, where the elite could gather to dine, dance, and socialize with people of equal status. The photographs showing the cottagers' residences and amusements make it clear that by the mid-1890s an exclusive resort had replaced the more democratic community of the Hotel Era.

Many cottagers would argue that the island's permanent residents also benefited from these changes, and in many ways, this was true. Almost all villagers had jobs providing services and goods to cottagers, which increased their own prosperity. High taxes and donations from wealthy cottagers supported and improved local schools, a well-stocked library, a fire department and hospital, and a number of beautiful churches.

Though newspaper editorials raised concerns about Bar Harbor's sole dependence on tourism as early as the 1890s, no other options were pursued. In fact, a group of farsighted summer residents organized the Hancock County Trustees of Public Reservations to protect land on the island from further development. Within thirty years, these lands and more would become Acadia National Park, drawing additional vacationers to the island and cementing the island's identity as a tourist destination.

In the period around World War I, several socioeconomic changes began that over the next three decades would drastically change Bar Harbor's character. Some of the

7

Photo courtesy of the Maine Historic Preservation Commission

cottagers who had sought a tranquil summer life in Bar Harbor now found its flurry of extravagant social activity to be excessive and moved to other resorts, such as nearby Northeast Harbor or Seal Harbor. As the early cottagers passed on, so too did the tradition of summering in one location. Their children would still summer on the island, but for shorter periods. The introduction of the national income tax in 1913 reduced the elite's disposable income. Wages for household help increased after World War I, making the large palaces of Bar Harbor's heyday more expensive to maintain. For the nation's middle class, however, the 1920s were a time of increasing prosperity. Not only did they have more money and time for vacations, but the popularity of the automobile introduced a new custom called touring—visiting several spots during a holiday. This change spurred demand for affordable accommodations, and roadside cabins and small restaurants began to spring up along popular routes.

The Depression did not impact the middle class in Bar Harbor as hard as in other areas, because their wealthy summer patrons continued to frequent their shops and use their services, albeit at a reduced level. The islanders' independent and adaptable nature helped them sustain themselves through this difficult period. America's entry into the Second World War in 1941 brought the greatest change to the island as gasoline and tire rationing reduced the number of summer visitors. Many islanders went off to fight in the war or to work in factories building armaments. Women who had never worked off the island went away to work and resisted doing domestic or farm work when they returned.

These employment shifts reduced the island's domestic work force, leaving wealthy land owners with reduced staff to run their mansions, making it difficult to maintain such large estates. Some of the large cottages were sold or rented, but even renting out these white elephants became difficult. During the 1930s and early 1940s, the Pulitzers and several other families tore down their palaces with the intention of building smaller summer cottages either in Bar Harbor or elsewhere. A few others simply abandoned their homes, allowing them to deteriorate. There were, however, some cottagers during this period who continued summering in Bar Harbor, enjoying a whirlwind social life at the Kebo Valley Club and the Bar Harbor Club, sailing, hiking, and picnicking.

On that fateful week in October 1947 when a fire raged across the eastern side of Mount Desert Island, some cottagers were relieved to have their oversized cottages destroyed, while for others it was a devastating blow. Only a few years later, the community had lost almost half of its cottages, the number shrinking from close to two hundred in 1912 to approximately one hundred in 1948. The *Bar Harbor Times* cottages list also shows that almost half of the remaining cottages were owned by single women: widows, divorcees, or spinsters. The last chapter of this book shows how the character of the community changed as residents adapted to a Bar Harbor that was by then attracting a more democratic population of visitors, much like the rusticators of the 1870s.

In this postwar period, some year-round and summer residents organized a company to purchase the Mount Desert Reading Room, renovating and expanding it into what is now the Bar Harbor Inn. Many of the grand estates that once lined Eden Street were replaced with motels and later, modern hotels. The sacrifice of one of Bar Harbor's most splendid palaces for the Bluenose ferry terminal became one of the key measures reviving the town's economy. Day trippers waiting for the ferry, or those who had disembarked, would stop in town for a few hours and patronize the local shops. Grocers who had once solely served cottagers now began making sandwiches for these tourists. With these developments, Bar Harbor adapted to a new type of tourism.

Fortunately, the corncob-filled mattresses of the earliest boarding houses have been replaced with firm, comfortable beds, and a broad selection of gourmet delights has replaced the earlier staples of fish and potatoes. One thing has not changed: the opportunity to explore the diverse beauty of Mount Desert Island.

Photo courtesy of the Maine Historic Preservation Commission

The Island Settlers

LIKE THE SUMMER SOJOURNERS who would follow in later years, William Lynam was attracted to Mount Desert Island for its abundant resources and beauty. The island offered plenty for making a living in nineteenth-century Maine: lumber for building ships, houses, boxes, and furniture; water to power the mills and navigate to other ports for trade; fertile soil to grow food; and fish for eating and selling. A blacksmith by trade, Lynam moved with his wife, Hannah Tracey, from Gouldsboro, Maine, to the island in 1831 and built this modest homestead at Schooner Head. Over time, this homestead would be described as "lonely" and "not specially picturesque" by famous artists who boarded there, but who nevertheless made it their temporary home during their sojourns on the island.

Photo courtesy of the Maine Historic Preservation Commission

LYNAM WAS A subsistence farmer like many of his fellow islanders, producing enough pork, lamb, dairy products, and vegetables to feed his wife and nine children. During the Civil War, islanders set up oil presses such as this one in which menhaden—also called pogies—were boiled and pressed to produce oil. For a few short years, the oil sold for $1.25 a gallon, five times its prewar price, before overfishing depleted the resource in this area. Women assisted in the process by "knitting" (netting) pogy nets, sometimes making thousands of knots over the course of many days to create a two-inch-mesh net, two hundred to five hundred feet long by eighteen feet deep.

Photo courtesy of the Maine Historic Preservation Commission

THIS WATER WHEEL was an important source of power in the nineteenth century. Lynam would cut down trees in early spring and haul them back to his water-powered sawmill with a team of oxen. He cut the wood into lumber, shingles, spool blocks (for vessels), and other products to sell in local and national markets. Besides the homestead and mill, Lynam's hundred-acre farm at Schooner Head included two oxen, two cows, a young horse, and twelve sheep.

According to common lore, sailors called the area Schooner Head because they said that in the fog, the pale stone of the headland resembled the white sails of a schooner.

Photo courtesy of the Maine Historic Preservation Commission

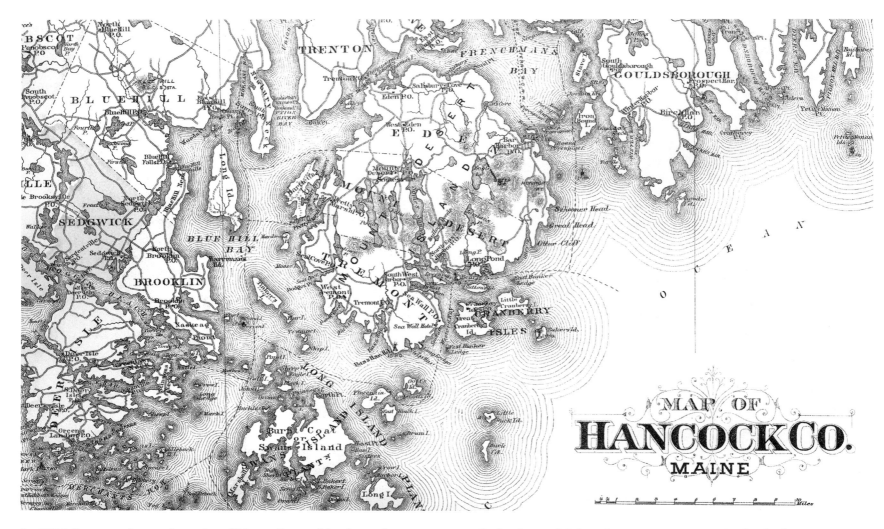

MAP OF HANCOCK CO. MAINE

IN 1796, EDEN, as the northern tier of Mount Desert Island was then called, separated from the southern district of Mount Desert. The names of the early families—Thomas, Roberts, Higgins, Rodick, Salsbury, Young, Hamor, and Lynam—are still prevalent on its shores today. These pioneers established their homes in this sheltered northern nook for good reason; its location and deep harbors protected coasting vessels that came to bring goods to the community or to take lumber and fish to faraway ports. In 1796, Eden had 88 voting (male) residents, 35 houses, 24 barns, 14 horses, 62 oxen, 222 cows and steers, and 123 swine. Historian Richard Hale concluded that with about two men and two oxen per house, Eden families built their wealth on lumber, not market crops, though every family grew their own food, made their own butter and cheese, and fished to survive.

Map courtesy of the Maine Historic Preservation Commission

BEFORE THE EUROPEANS settled Mount Desert Island, people of the Passamaquoddy, Penobscot, Micmac, and Maliseet tribes would summer on Pemetic (the Native American term for Mount Desert Island, which translates as "a range of mountains"). They would set up their camps on Bar Island and at Hulls Cove, Cromwell Harbor, and the fields on lower Bridge Street, as shown in this 1870s photo. Their summer days were spent fishing, digging clams, hunting small game, and collecting berries, roots, sweetgrass, and birch bark. In 1883, 250 Native Americans settled in camps around Bar Harbor for the summer, erecting forty tents along the shore at the foot of Holland Avenue. In September, they returned to their inland homes.

Photo courtesy of the Maine Historic Preservation Commission

IN PRE-TWENTIETH-CENTURY TIMES, Native American culture revolved around hunting, but when European settlers encroached on their territory with their own hunting and logging activities, the Indians were forced to change their ways. Summering along the Bar Harbor shore, the male Indians found that they could sell their birch-bark canoes, teach sojourners the art of canoeing, and help gather materials for canoes and baskets. As tourists became more interested in Indian culture, the market for baskets and other goods increased, allowing many tribal women to become the major wage earners in their families.

Photo courtesy of the Maine Historic Preservation Commission

VISITING THIS Wabanaki family's tent in the 1880s, a tourist described what he found in the half-tent booths: ". . . draperies of red and blue and orange calico, or bunting. Broad shelves, serving as counters, presented a charming medley of harmonious colors. Baskets of every shape and tint are piled into glowing masses. Seal-skins and deer-skins, pipes and sticks fashioned from distorted roots, canoes and paddles great and small, snow shoes, lacrosse-bats, bows and arrows, moccasins and caps— what do not their skilful [sic] fingers put into captivating guise to witch away the money of the idler? Then there are gulls' breasts and wings, stuffed owls, pearly grebe plumage, and, their latest novelties, wood-baskets and flower pots of birch-bark, etched with a frieze of native scenes."[1]

Photo courtesy of the Maine Historic Preservation Commission

GREETINGS FROM PICTURESQUE AMERICA

Arthur Livingston, Publisher, New York. 413

THE INDIAN VILLAGE, BAR HARBOR, ME.

AN 1882 BAR HARBOR newspaper headline—WHERE SHOULD THE INDIANS GO THIS SUMMER?—illustrates the tension that was developing between the Native Americans and those prospering from the summer resort trade. With Bar Harbor's increasing exclusiveness, some in the community felt that it was unsightly for the Indian camps to line the shore, although others still supported their presence. The compromise was to build a small community for the Indians in Squaw Hollow, a derogatory term for the lane adjacent to where the YWCA resides today. Rusticator Marian Peabody described her visits there: "We used to go from tent to tent, buying sweet-smelling baskets and admiring the cunning children and papooses." Several times during the summers, the Indians would share their dances and ceremonial customs through exhibits and performances.

Photo courtesy of the Maine Historic Preservation Commission

17

THE TOWN OF EDEN was known for its shipbuilders. One could find the Hamor, Higgins, and Brewer families engaged in building vessels in the sheltered coves of Frenchman Bay. Between 1809 and 1889, approximately 125 vessels were built in Eden. Some were built for fishing expeditions to local areas or lengthy sails to St. Georges Bay, depriving the families of their men for months at a time. Other boats were built for the coasting trade, taking lumber, hay, and other marketable goods to East Coast cities and returning with molasses, salt, sand, rope, and other items not produced on Mount Desert Island.

Building a boat could take as little as two months, depending on its size, and various specialized work crews would travel between yards, performing the necessary tasks. Before the Civil War, almost every man went to sea at least once, either for fishing or coasting.

Photo courtesy of the Maine Historic Preservation Commission

"IN THE OLDEN DAYS . . . a man who owned a fairly good wood lot, situated not too far away from a good landing, together with a yoke of oxen, was considered well to do, especially if he had also two or three strong sons."[2] In the 1860s there were six sawmills on the island, similar to this one located at Duck Brook. Each spring, local lumbermen would fell trees, float them downstream to the mills, and saw the logs into lumber to build ships, houses, boxes, and shingles. Oak, rock maple, and, later, white pine, were plentiful and used for plank decks on schooners and rails.

Photo courtesy of the Maine Historic Preservation Commission

THESE MEN at McFarland's farm by Eagle Lake probably agreed with Albert L. Higgins's comments about early days on the island: "I like the fall because I could hunt the partridges and coots and other game, and the winter because of its long and pleasant winter evenings and then too, I could coast [sled] and go skating. The springtime brought us the greater amount of hard work like sawing and splitting and piling up wood. I always dreaded the summer, because of the hayraking and the thunderstorms. Indeed, I have raked over the eleven-acre field, now known as Albert Meadow, and the Village Green many, many times."[3] In 1861, John McFarland not only owned this two-hundred-acre farm, complete with two oxen, one colt, eleven sheep, and one pig, but also was part owner of three sailing vessels and a mill. Unlike many of his fellow farmers, he also owned a carriage, considered a luxury in those days.

Photo courtesy of the Maine Historic Preservation Commission

In 1872, the *Ellsworth American* reported on the status of farming in Eden: "The potato harvest is bad . . . Most farmers have raised enough for their consumption. A few will sell enough to pay their taxes." Most farming on the island provided enough food and clothing for families, but little more. Families such as Willard Fogg's, shown here, kept some sheep to produce wool, one or two hogs, and a cow or two for butter, cheese, and milk in the summer months. Vegetables would be harvested in the fall and stored in cellars or outdoor pits, and fish would be caught year-round, then dried and salted for the family's table.

This photograph, taken at a later date, shows multiple types of wagons used for farming. The jigger wagon (at left) was sturdy enough to haul heavy barrels, while the next one to the right is a general-purpose cart, a spring wagon. A buggy, the next one to the right, provided passenger transport, while deliveries could be made in the depot wagon (at far right).

SOMETIME AROUND 1900, these thirty-four Grand Army of the Republic soldiers gathered for a reunion in Bar Harbor to share songs and stories of their Civil War experiences. Gray-haired at this point, they vividly remembered their regiments. Though many of these men were experienced seamen, only eleven joined the navy, according to Eden historian Eben Hamor. Eighteen joined the 26th Maine Regiment, and about the same number enlisted with the 1st Maine Heavy Artillery. In total, eighty-nine young boys and men enlisted, and fifteen served as substitutes out of a total population of around 1,100. At least a quarter of these husbands, fathers, and sons never came home. This was especially true for the Zaccheus Higgins family. Five sons of this Cromwell Harbor resident went off to war, and only one returned.

Photo courtesy of the James M. Parker Post, American Legion

TOBIAS ROBERTS epitomized the Bar Harbor pioneer's dominant characteristic: adaptability. Tobias and Mary Roberts moved from Boston to settle in Bar Harbor in 1836, opening a little red store on the shore that served mariners and fishermen. In the 1850s, before the Civil War, he saw an opportunity for a new type of industry for the island: tourism. As shipbuilding and fishing began to wane in the 1870s, Roberts and other visionary islanders decided it was time to transition to their new occupation.

Photo courtesy of Raymond Strout

Rusticators

THE HUDSON RIVER SCHOOL painters who visited Mount Desert Island in the decades before the Civil War were the first to capture its natural beauty on canvas and share it with the public through art galleries and salons. One of the artists' favorite vantage points was the dramatic view from Green Mountain (now called Cadillac), toward Otter Creek. Nowhere else on the East Coast can this combination of mountain and sea be found, and image makers wanted to capture it on canvas or in photographs.

Photo courtesy of the Maine Historic Preservation Commission

WHEN NOTED ARTISTS first visited the island, they were struck by the variety of scenic experiences available to them. The sweeping grandeur of Green Mountain's vistas contrasted with more pastoral coastal scenes like this one at Hulls Cove. The quiet coves where shipbuilders had constructed coastal schooners, were now becoming havens for canoeists and boaters. Nineteenth-century Americans were beginning to learn that vacations were not just for the elite; they could also be valuable for the health of the middle class as well.

Photo courtesy of the Bar Harbor Historical Society

LONG DRESSES did not deter Victorian women from hiking up mountains or visiting even the most rugged sections of the coastline. Known as the Ovens, these rock formations on the east side of the island were described by Clara Barnes Martin in her 1874 guidebook as "bold arches with zigzag moldings, in the depths of which the old Romanesque builders placed their doorways." As tourists, artists, and geologists discovered these remote destinations, they soon became popular spots for picnics, even at night, with the "moon lighting the grim cliff behind, or the ruddy glow of bonfires flashing up under the dark arches," according to Martin.

Photo courtesy of the Maine Historic Preservation Commission

FREDERICK E. CHURCH was the most noted pupil of Thomas Cole, nineteenth-century founder of the Hudson River School of landscape painting. Church followed his mentor Cole to Mount Desert, where both of them captured the coastal and mountain scenery of the island. Caroline Chesebro, a newspaper columnist for New York's *The Independent*, visited the island in 1865 and wrote of her experience: "[W]e reached a hight [sic] which commanded Newport mountain, Spout'n Horn, beds and walls of rock and the blue ocean with its ever changing lights and glory . . . and its broad unbroken expanse . . . and our wonder ended that Church should have come here, year by year, from boyhood up to manhood, and that all artists love the place."[1] Artists were among the first visitors to the island, and before the establishment of boardinghouses and inns, they stayed with island families, soaking up Yankee culture along with the breathtaking views.

AT THE MIDPOINT of the nineteenth century, American artists were experimenting with painting bold, natural scenes, such as rugged rocks and crashing seas. Having seen Cole's sketches of the Maine coastal wilderness and having read Henry David Thoreau's accounts of inland Maine, Church headed off on his inaugural visit in July 1850. He was not disappointed. "We were out on the rocks and peaks all day. It was a stirring sight to see the immense rollers come toppling in, changing their forms and gathering in bulk, then dashing into sparkling foam against the base of old 'Schooner Head,' and leaping a hundred feet into the air."[2] During his three months on the island, Church sketched and painted, producing many works like this one of a lumber mill. As his paintings began to circulate in urban art galleries, they sparked interest in this beautiful place that many Americans had never seen. Soon the word was out, and vacationers put the island on their list of destinations.

In the 1870s, photographer E. L. Allen captured this artist duo sketching in the open air. The *Ellsworth American* from August 11, 1870, reported, "The artists are scattered far and wide thru-out [sic] the country now. A good lady hailed a pair of them the other day as they were passing her house, fully equipped for sun or rain, and asked if they mended parasols and umbrellas, which reminds the *NY Post* that Mr. Church was once accosted by an old lady who inquired if he had any 'nice peppermint.' He answered, 'No, but I have some fresh chrome yellow.'"

Photo courtesy of the Maine Historic Preservation Commission

IN ADDITION to artists, many photographers were attracted to Bar Harbor, making images of both the island's natural beauty and its visitors. Augusta photographer Henry Bailey and his brother-in-law A. F. Morse of Hallowell (shown standing on the steps) set up this tintype tent for several seasons in downtown Bar Harbor in the 1880s and 1890s. They provided summer visitors with low-cost souvenir photographs prior to the availability of individual snapshot cameras.

Photo courtesy of the Maine Historic Preservation Commission

BAR HARBOR NATIVE Albert L. Higgins recalled this scene from the years just after the Civil War. General J. C. Caldwell, from nearby Ellsworth, acquired about a hundred "no longer needed" army tents and pitched them for July and August in Stephen Higgins's grassy field near where the Bar Harbor Inn stands today. Thus, Caldwell became one of Bar Harbor's first marketing agents, inviting the Hale, Emery, Prentiss, and Peters families from Bangor, Ellsworth, Blue Hill, and other nearby towns, many of whom would return in subsequent summers.

Croquet was a popular activity then; Higgins pointed out that one would find wickets set up in all available spaces. Though there is less open space today, one can still find people "sending" others' croquet balls in Bar Harbor.

Photo courtesy of the Maine Historic Preservation Commission

In 1855, Tobias Roberts built Bar Harbor's first hotel, the Agamont House, seen here as the vernacular Greek Revival building on the left. Prior to that date, he and his wife Mary had housed visiting rusticators in their home, offering them simple accommodations: corncob mattresses and hearty meals of fish and potatoes. The couple also ran a general store selling marine goods to coasting vessels and staples to islanders. Soon after the Civil War, "Uncle Tobe" expanded the Agamont House with the building on the right, and moved his store into the basement.

In August 1860, a stock company that apparently owned an island in Frenchman Bay held a meeting at the hotel and agreed that the firm's dividends should be a glass of ale and a bunch of turnips. This was a surprising decision since Maine had prohibited the manufacture and sale of alcohol in 1851.

Photo courtesy of the Maine Historic Preservation Commission

By 1883, ROBERTS responded to a growing tourist population by enlarging the original Greek Revival building into a two-story structure with third-floor dormers. Though the space had been expanded, the rooms and board remained simple, according to newspaper accounts. Many of the mattresses were still stuffed with corncobs, and one columnist begged for the proprietor to serve beef or something other than fish. The wide, covered porch jutting out from the hotel offered a pleasant place to spend a hot summer day.

Roberts also provided entertainment for rainy or foggy days. In the 1860s, he asked neighbor Stephen Higgins to build a double-track bowling alley by the shore. Island boys earned money setting up the pins for the players, keeping the boys employed and the visitors happy.

Photo courtesy of the Maine Historic Preservation Commission

THE ATTIRE worn by this gentleman hiker exemplifies the simple life sought by rusticators in the 1870s. The flannel walking suit, sturdy boots, and brimmed hat protected him from both cold and sun as he rambled through the lowlands to this secluded spot at the base of Newport Mountain. He could rest here before making the steep climb up the mountain, sustained by tasty blueberries. According to a newspaper account of the time, "After a day spent fishing or climbing, we sit around the blazing fireplace and recount the day's adventures, and pity our unfortunate fellow creatures who are enduring the pitiless suns and unrefreshing nights of New York."[3]

Photo courtesy of the Maine Historic Preservation Commission

DESPITE THEIR FORMAL-LOOKING Victorian attire, these visitors didn't hesitate to clamber on the island's shores, exploring the bold rock formations just as naturalist Louis Agassiz had done in years prior. It was during this mid-nineteenth-century period that the science of geology captured the imagination of the American public. As new interest developed in natural wonders, Mount Desert attracted scientists such as Agassiz and John James Audubon. In 1865, the U.S. Geological Survey built a shack at the summit of Green Mountain from which to map the coastal region.

Science continues to play a role on the island today, with two scientific institutes situated there.

Photo courtesy of the Maine Historic Preservation Commission

Traveling to Mount Desert Island in the 1850s was an arduous adventure. Visitors from Boston took a train to Portland, followed by voyages on two or three coastal vessels before finally reaching Southwest Harbor. From there, a three-and-a-half-hour wagon ride would take them to Eden, as Bar Harbor was then known. Alternatively, visitors could take a stagecoach from Belfast over bumpy, dusty roads and over the Trenton toll bridge, built in 1836, to arrive in Bar Harbor.

Just after Tobias Roberts enlarged his wharf in 1868, William Lawrence arrived and described the village, as seen in this photograph: ". . . where [there] are now Cottage and West Streets were rough field and bog, brilliant in July with wild roses. From the plain one could see the whole sweep of mountains, a view now shut off by shade trees and houses . . . There were no fences, no lawns, no gardens or estates. The whole island was ours."[4]

Photo courtesy of the Maine Historic Preservation Commission

THOUGH MOST STEAMERS made only occasional stops, Captain Charles Deering put his steamer *Lewiston*, a 246-foot side-wheeler, on a regular schedule for twice-a-week landings at Bar Harbor beginning in 1869. For the following decade, Deering had a monopoly on regular service to Bar Harbor in the summers, at times transporting four hundred to five hundred passengers at once, according to an article in the March 1, 1934, edition of the *Bar Harbor Times*.

When the steamer arrived at the Roberts wharf, it was a noted event. Many local people and visitors would saunter down to greet the incoming guests and wave good-bye to those departing. The passengers were in good hands with Deering. He had grown up on boats between Portland and Machias and was known as a man of "skill and experience, quiet and self-possessed, yet with an eye to the perfection of every department of his boat."[5]

Photo courtesy of the Maine Historic Preservation Commission

DRESSED IN THEIR "Martha Washington" costumes with ruffled caps and modesty capes draped over their shoulders, these Bar Harbor visitors showed their patriotic fervor as they celebrated the centennial of the Battle of Bunker Hill on August 23, 1875. Still recuperating from the Civil War, and eager to forget the country's economic woes, people sought ways to commemorate the historic occasion. Costume parties, parades, and speeches, delivered in character, were common in the Northeast. All the participants in the photograph had to remain still and serious in order for the photographer to capture this milestone in our nation's history.

Photo courtesy of the Maine Historic Preservation Commission

DAVID RODICK JR. grew up on Bar Island and made his living as a sea captain and weir fisherman. He and his wife, Betsey Brewer, took in boarders prior to the Civil War. In 1866 they built the modest hotel shown at right in this photograph, facing the newly constructed Main Street. Each year, the number of visitors increased, easing the financial strains that came from disappointments in the lumbering and coasting trades.

By 1868 the *Ellsworth American* claimed, "Bar Harbor is multiplying hotel accommodations almost as rapidly as the Athenians did their Gods." Responding to this surge, David Rodick and his sons, Fountain and Serenus, built the mansard-roofed "Siamese Twin" addition in 1873, with room for 350 guests. The newspaper once observed that old Captain Rodick "seems to keep [a] hotel chiefly for the pleasure of entertaining his fellow creatures, so genial, kindly and accommodating is he in all his ways."

Photo courtesy of the Maine Historic Preservation Commission

By 1881, VACATIONERS were arriving faster than accommodations could be built. Rodick and Sons responded with this massive Queen Anne–style establishment, soon to be known as one of the best society hotels in America. The clientele was consistent, so everyone recognized each other. The twice-weekly hops (dances) were popular, attracting more than three thousand people at times.

This hotel was the first major architectural commission for John E. Clark, an architect-builder from Ellsworth through which he made his local reputation. This six-story, four-hundred-room hotel featured plenty of spaces for socializing, including a seventy-by-thirty-foot parlor, a music room twice that size, a broad piazza "affording a noble promenade," and a lobby, which became known as "the fish pond" for its matchmaking possibilities. The hotel's architectural centerpiece, a ninety-foot octagonal tower, commanded a view of sea and mountains.

Photo courtesy of the Maine Historic Preservation Commission

THIS SPACIOUS, functional dining room at the Rodick served meals not only to the hotel guests, but also to "mealers," cottagers who took their meals in hotels. One of the early chefs, Fred Jellison of Ellsworth, reported cooking more than 750 meals a day. Gone were the meals of yesteryear, which consisted mainly of fish, potatoes, and Indian pudding. The Rodick's manager kept the larder well supplied with a wide variety of meats, fruits, and vegetables. Over time, the demand for local produce prompted the development of new farms and greenhouses. Families who had abandoned farming in the past took it up again in the name of tourism.

Photo courtesy of the Bar Harbor Historical Society

RUNNING A HOTEL such as the Rodick required chambermaids, butlers, chefs, waitresses, kitchen help, clerks, and managers—a total of 180 people. In this photo, three-quarters of the staff are gathered on the hotel steps, along with a friendly canine. Bonnie lasses from the local area would don their cambric dresses and starched white aprons to wait tables.

Serving elite members of society would often try the patience of the staff. One proprietor lamented that he was "besieged with letters from parties wishing to rent the best rooms at the cheapest rates, or an elderly lady wanting a corner room on the first floor with a good ocean and mountain view, a fireplace, near an elevator, and, of course, far away from any men or children . . . they make such a noise!"[6]

Photo courtesy of the Bar Harbor Historical Society

JOHN A. RODICK, one of David Jr.'s thirteen siblings, operated this smaller hotel, the Birch Tree Inn, on Cottage Street, where the post office stands today. Some of these smaller hotels operated independently of the larger ones, whereas others were cottages associated with the larger hotels. The sojourners in this circa 1870s photo are playing lawn tennis (at right), while the spectators relax on the veranda. A low-slung two-seater buckboard is being readied by the house to take guests on a ride to Schooner Head to see the famous Anemone Cave, a popular excursion of the day. For the evening's entertainment, there were many options: hops at the hotels, musical concerts, or "a grand mass bowling match . . . with the sudden appearance of the 'fortune teller,' whose name as deciphered by one of the party was 'gorgeous belle.'"[7]

Photo courtesy of the Maine Historic Preservation Commission

IN 1880, TWO MONTHS after Theodore Roosevelt (front row, center) proposed to his future wife, Alice Lee (to his right), they joined with several of his Harvard classmates for a studio pose to remember their vacation. From the very beginning, Bar Harbor attracted prominent New York, Boston, and Philadelphia families to the island. Many of them, like the Minots and Welds, were among the first to build simple cottages and return year after year, attracting other family members to build cottages as well. The others in this photo include Henry B. Chapin (front row right), Henry Shaw (behind Roosevelt), and Rose Saltonstall (back left). Sisters Grace and Alice Rathbone, identically dressed in black, are smiling at solemn Richard Saltonstall (back middle) and Minot Weld (back right).

HISTORIAN CLEVELAND AMORY described Walter Roberts's Newport House as a place where one could walk and talk, and many congregated in front of this Bar Harbor resort, built in 1869. Bar Harbor's hotels served as meeting places for fashionable society. Socialites would gather on piazzas, benches, and chairs around the lawns, chatting with each other and making plans for their next adventure. During this era, Bar Harbor was known for its lack of conventionality. "It is one of the charms of the place. There is no elaborateness of dress or equipage nor display of any kind," wrote an *Ellsworth American* correspondent in 1873.[8]

Photo courtesy of the Maine Historic Preservation Commission

"WE PUSH OFF from the wharf and its throng of laughing, chattering people all waiting eagerly for their boat. The bay is very calm and the waves reflect the gold and purple tints of the clouds so vividly that we at once feel the truth of the epithet, 'opalescent,' so often used in describing them. We move lazily along, there is no need for haste—that belongs to a world far from this. We have escaped from the sound of steam whistle and the factory bell, are here to enjoy the *dolce far niente*, and as nearly as possible, we approach delectable condition when the body is at perfect rest."[9] Quite often, an excursion on the bay would follow a trek to the top of Green Mountain and back, a ten-mile round-trip. Early diaries recount days filled with adventures; Mount Desert's rusticators came to enjoy nature, and they did it to the fullest.

Photo courtesy of the Maine Historic Preservation Commission

Canoeing became another popular pastime for the rusticators. Maine Native Americans promoted the sport by crafting sturdy canoes, offering lessons in paddling techniques, and guiding sojourners on tours. Placid canoe excursions on the island's many lakes were just as popular as the organized canoe parades and races. In the 1880s, Mr. George Baldwin Newell helped to organize a canoe club. By 1888, interest had grown sufficiently to warrant the construction of a clubhouse and boat pier at Bar Island on land leased from Daniel Rodick. The receptions held there a few times each summer became as popular as the parades and races, and they soon outgrew the small clubhouse. "Of course the annual regatta was the club's most important event, where one could enter such classes as mixed doubles, and double sculls. There was always one Indian race, when these experts with paddles could show off their skills."[10]

Canoe Parade at Bar Harbor

Photo courtesy of the Maine Historic Preservation Commission

Newport Camp at Eagle Lake was built to provide shelter for patrons waiting to hire a rowboat or canoe. The two-mile-long lake, just over two miles from Bar Harbor, "had double attractions. Every rod of its shores is a study for the artist, while the sportsman may catch all the trout he desires."[11] Artist Frederick Church named the lake after seeing eagles soaring over its waters.

Photo courtesy of the Maine Historic Preservation Commission

JUST AS GREEN MOUNTAIN attracted sojourners to its peak, it also lured entrepreneurs eager to bring in more visitors and make money at the same time. The stern-wheeled steamer *Wauwinet* was part of one such enterprise begun by solicitor Frank H. Clergue and fellow Bangor businessmen. By 1883, he put his plan into action: passengers could take a twenty-minute horse-drawn buckboard ride from the Bar Harbor village to the north end of Eagle Lake, followed by a twenty-minute cruise on the *Wauwinet* down the lake to an eastern shore landing, where they would be transferred to a cog railroad for the thirty-minute ascent to the Green Mountain summit.

Photo courtesy of the Maine Historic Preservation Commission

ONE OF THE BUILDERS of Clergue's cog railroad described the climb as "no trip for those who were nervously inclined," as the steep inclines in certain spots made the passenger feel as though the car would topple over. As the car strained on a steep grade, one hefty passenger asked the conductor what their fate would be if the cogs should break. "Looking down into the clear blue waters of Eagle Lake which lay right below them, he replied earnestly: 'Well, ma'am, that depends on what kind of a life you've been living before you came on board this car." Despite these anxieties, brave passengers were rewarded with a stunning panoramic view from the summit for their $2.50 round-trip fare.

Photo courtesy of the Maine Historic Preservation Commission

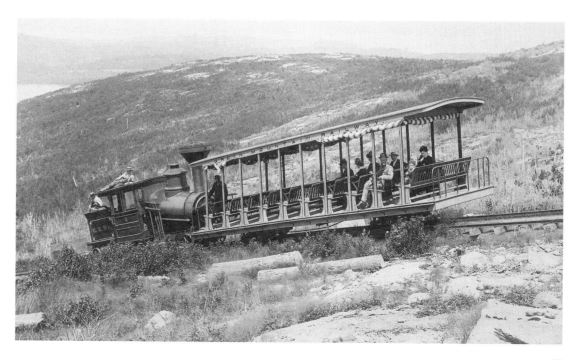

"FROM THE BOLD BLUFF in front of the house, the beholder can see the base of the mountains resting on the seas, and frequently five hundred sail of mackerel and haddock catchers can be counted from that outlook!"[12] A building had stood at the peak of the island's highest mountain since 1855. By 1883, Clergue had replaced a modest hotel, built in 1866 by Daniel Brewer, with this elegant Queen Anne–style inn offering twenty-six rooms, meals, parlors for a rest, and a glass observatory for views of the Cranberry Isles, Mount Desert Rock, and the vast ocean beyond.

Within three years, close to eight thousand passengers had made the trip on the cog railway, but ridership quickly declined once the Green Mountain Carriage Road Company, organized by Bar Harbor merchants Elihu and Ralph Hamor and John Carr, opened a new avenue to the summit in 1888. Buckboard drivers hailed the new road and were soon making profits.

Ironically, the ultimate result of the inn atop Green Mountain was to convince many summer visitors that the mountaintops should be preserved in their natural state, spurring the creation of Acadia National Park.

STYLING THEIR TABLEAU after Renoir's famous 1881 painting, *Luncheon of the Boating Party*, this group has set aside their lawn tennis rackets for a lovely picnic on a fine day in 1884. Teatime is complete with a trio of wine bottles, some good bread and jam, and homemade pickles.

Prior to this, the *Mount Desert Herald*, the island's first newspaper, began reporting all the society activities. As one correspondent noted, by the early 1880s, "Bar Harbor was settling into a quiet elegance." No longer were calico dresses and flannel shirts acceptable. In fact, ladies needed three or more dresses for their daytime entertainments. "High teas, dinner parties and all sorts of excursions left no-idle moment."[13]

Photo courtesy of the William Otis Sawtelle Collections, Acadia National Park

"HANDKERCHIEFS WAVED and salutatory cheers arose as the steamer *Sappho* pulled into port. The arrival always brought groups of people down to the wharf to see who would be arriving on that day, or who would be leaving."[14] Once train service had been extended to the mainland in 1884, the Maine Central Railroad built this speedy steamer to make summer runs between Bar Harbor and the Mount Desert Ferry railhead in Hancock on the mainland. Built in 1885, the 161-foot *Sappho* offered an alternative route to the island, competing with the three established steamer lines that carried passengers by water from Boston and New York.

CAPTAIN EDGAR P. DICKSON (front row, third from right) and his *Sappho* crew provided a safe and comfortable ride across Frenchman Bay for their summer passengers. Each man had his job. Firemen Leonard McAvery and Thomas Dickson stoked the appetites of four massive boilers, six feet in length. Engineer Porter Smith of Ellsworth maintained every part of her machinery, assisted by Fred Hutchins. Phillip Seavey, the mate, took care of the freight, "as though a consignor traveled with it," noted the *Bar Harbor Record* of May 22, 1895. Two men had the most contact with passengers: "the ever vigilant purser, Freeman Higgins, a Bar Harbor native," and Manuel Roderick, the black porter, who "was a favorite with both crew and passengers, always obliging and good natured, as ready to help an ill-dressed woman with a family of crying children . . . as he is to go to the assistance of the millionaire's family."[15]

PASSENGERS COULD RELAX in the rich, velvet-upholstered chairs and benches of the *Sappho*'s main saloon, located on the upper deck. Lined with windows, the spacious cabin afforded a splendid view of Frenchman Bay. A broad staircase led down to a lower cabin where ladies could rest in their own elegant saloon, bright with white walls and gold trim. For weary travelers on the last leg of their trip to Mount Desert, comfort was a key commodity for the weary travelers.

Photo courtesy of the Maine Historic Preservation Commission

THE ATLANTIC HOUSE, a modest hotel built by J. H. Douglas in 1870, burned in 1873 and was rebuilt on a larger scale. It was purchased in 1887 by two Boston ladies, the Misses Balch, who were experienced in catering to society. With practiced hands, the Misses redecorated the hotel, renamed it the Louisburg, revised the menu, and raised the rates from $4 to $5 per day.

Photo courtesy of the Maine Historic Preservation Commission

EVENING HOTEL LIFE depended on dances, musicales, and concerts to keep society on its toes. Some members of the Boston Symphony spent their summers playing concerts at the Louisburg. With an eclectic assortment of furnishings, from velvet-clad Victorian chairs to cozy sofas and rattan chairs, the Louisburg's music room attracted plenty of visitors in the evening. It was just the place to socialize with friends, initiate a summer romance, and maybe even become betrothed. Reviewing the social season of 1882, a reporter commented, "Many pleasant acquaintances were made. . . . some few fortunate ones have already met their fate. Many others are fast nearing theirs. . . . As regards to entertainments, receptions and musicales, the season of 1882 [was] surprisingly brilliant."[16]

Photo courtesy of the Maine Historic Preservation Commission

LOUISBURG GUESTS could greet their social callers in a small parlor like the one at left, simply furnished with a comfortable sofa, rattan chair, and a few upholstered chairs. On chilly, foggy days, families could gather around their parlor fire to read or share stories of their island adventures, and to make plans for their next excursions.

Dinner.

SOUP.	Mutton Broth. Clam Chowder.
FISH.	Boiled Salmon, Anchovie Sauce.
BOILED.	Leg of Mutton, Caper Sauce. Corned Beef. Tongue. Fowl and Pork.
ROAST.	Turkey, Giblet Sauce. Spring Lamb, Mint Sauce. Rib of Beef, Dish Gravy.
COLD.	Corned Beef. Tongue. Ham. Potato Salad.
ENTREES.	Fricassee of Chicken. Currie of Mutton with Rice. Baked Macaroni with Cheese. Queen Fritters.

VEGETABLES	Mashed Potatoes. Boiled Potatoes. Green Peas. Asparagus. String Beans. New Beets. Cauliflower.
RELISHES.	Worcestershire Sauce. Olives. Walnut Ketchup. Tomato Ketchup. Mixed Pickles. Halford Sauce. Salad Dressing. Girkins. Cucumbers. Sliced Tomatoes.
PASTRY	Chocolate Pudding, Cream Sauce. Apple Pie. Rhubarb Pie. Custard Pie. Sunshine Cake. Pound Cake. Orange Cake. Spanish Meringues.
DESSERT.	English Walnuts. Filberts. Pecans. Almonds. Castanas. Raisins. Oranges Watermelon. Bananas. Vanilla Ice Cream.
TEA.	COFFEE.

JULY 10. 1887.

IN TYPICAL VICTORIAN FASHION, the dinner menu of the Louisburg offered a plethora of fish, meats, and poultry, and relatively few vegetables. By the late 1880s, Bar Harbor visitors were relieved of having to subsist on potatoes and fish, as earlier sojourners had done.

The publication of *Mrs. Beeton's Book of Household Management* helped middle- and upper-class women to improve the sophistication of their meals, as the Balch sisters had done for the Louisburg dinner fare. With the rise of the middle class, no longer was the noontime meal the largest; the evening meal, dinner, became the most important and a popular time for entertaining.

AN ANCIENT RELIC left over from glacial ages, Balance Rock lay just offshore from where Grant Park now stands, and was an ideal play spot for children. As Prall Grant Bacon described in 1937, "Bar Harbor was an enchanted world to a growing child, with the tide bringing in new treasures each day. The rocks on the beach lie in ledge formations so that fascinating shelves are made for imaginary pantries and kitchens. We used to stock them with the green seaweed for lettuce and mussels for oysters and countless other items that I have forgotten."

Photo courtesy of the Maine Historic Preservation Commission

IN AUGUST 1885, eight youthful visitors gathered on the Rodick Hotel lawn for this whimsical photograph. Young people from many large East Coast cities visited Bar Harbor under the watchful eyes of their parents. Mrs. Van Buren had brought her two daughters, Marian (perched on the water pump) and Bessie (on her right), to the island to escape the vile summer conditions in New York City. New Yorker physician Gaspar Griswold (front left) poses with his friend, Bostonian William Lawrence, who would later become the Episcopal bishop of Massachusetts. The others—Marian Linzee (back right), Mr. Cornell (catching the water), George Adams (far left), and Charles Whitney—enjoy the frolic.

Photo courtesy of the Bar Harbor Historical Society

IT WAS A BUSY TIME at the Maine Central Railroad wharf at Bar Harbor when both the nimble steamer *Mount Desert* and the far larger *Frank Jones* were discharging passengers and taking on new ones, along with loads of freight. It was a noisy place, with horse-drawn carts collecting passengers and trunks, and sometimes even horses and pianos. With passenger travel and freight transport significantly increasing each year, the MCRR had to build larger waiting rooms and express offices on the dock. Though fewer coasting schooners were visiting this bustling harbor by the 1880s, private yachts, boat rental businesses, and passenger steamers kept the harbor alive with activity.

Photo courtesy of the Maine Historic Preservation Commission

WHEN BUILT IN 1873, the Grand Central Hotel was advertised as the largest in Maine, a far cry from the humble hotel it had replaced—the Bay View House (Hamor, Young and Co., proprietors). Local builder W. A. Jordan designed this four-story, 100,000-square-foot hotel with piazzas, an observation tower, and two-tier balconies from which guests could see and be seen. Built to accommodate more than three hundred guests, this hotel tested the waters of grandness, offering concerts and balls to its guests and visitors, but just like the Green Mountain Railway, its popularity peaked and declined. By the late 1890s, it had been sold and demolished, the land turned into the popular Village Green.

Photo courtesy of the Bar Harbor Historical Society

BY AUGUST 1, 1872, David G. Haskins Jr. had spent twenty days exploring Mount Desert Island. One could picture him here, on his last day, as he wrote this account in his diary: "We had quite an elaborate dinner at Otter Creek. They built a fire and made coffee, scrambled eggs and fried potatoes. After dinner [lunch], we went to Thunder Hole and to the cliffs and rode home through the gorge by starlight."[15] A perfect end to a vacation.

Photo courtesy of the Maine Historic Preservation Commission

THIS BUSY WATERFRONT SCENE from around 1885 shows the extent of change that had occurred in the village since the 1860s. The Native American campsite at the far right is now surrounded by other buildings: minuscule houses for workers, called Peanut Row; the towering West End Hotel, offering "metropolitan" accommodations; warehouses for freight and merchandise; wharves where boaters could find rentals of all sorts; and, rising up on the hills, the cottages.

By this time, many of the hotel guests were building their own summer homes, giving rise to the Cottage Era and a subsequent decline in the hotel business. Many of the early rusticators complained of this change. As one remarked, "The delightful informal picnics, walks and excursions are abandoned and calling, dining, and dancing take their place."[16]

Photo courtesy of the Maine Historic Preservation Commission

The Cottage Era

According to local lore, Chatham, Massachusetts, resident Alpheus Hardy heard of Mount Desert's attractions from a traveling saleswoman who raved about the island's "thirteen mountain peaks, wooded glens, walks, drives, rocks and caves, headlands and coves, known only to a few."[1] In 1865, seeking a restful sojourn for his sons who were returning from the war, Hardy brought his family and his ward, Montgomery Sears, to Eden. There, they purchased land from their host, Captain Stephen Higgins, for $300. Two years later, the couple hired the Doane contracting firm of Boston to build this simple, picturesque structure. Named Birch Point, it was finished in 1868, complete with a generous veranda and sturdy benches from which to view the bay and watch the comings and goings in the harbor.

Photo courtesy of the Maine Historic Preservation Commission

Frustrated that his health would not allow him to study for the ministry, Alpheus Hardy had decided to make money for godly works through the merchant marine trade. He built swift coasting schooners in the 1840s and sent them worldwide for trade, producing a fortune for good works and leading to the creation of Alpheus Hardy & Co. Both he and his wife, Susan (née Holmes), were active supporters of educational institutions and religious enterprises. At his death in August 1887, the *Sandwich Observer* extolled, "His name was a tower of strength to every enterprise, and [he] was always an earnest religious worker," traits carried on by his four sons, Alpheus H., Edward, Charles, and Arthur.

Montgomery Sears, son of Hardy's partner, Joshua Sears, lived with the Hardys after his father's death and later built The Briars cottage in Bar Harbor in 1881.

Photo courtesy of the Congregational Library, Boston, Massachusetts

BY THE 1890S, BAR HARBOR cottages had grown in scale and formality. Mrs. Hardy had expanded Birch Point with extensions to the side and rear, as well as a wraparound porch. By this time, most cottagers were no longer taking their meals at nearby hotels. Instead, they had enlarged their summer homes with functional kitchens and larger dining rooms to better entertain their guests.

More than half a century later, the Bar Harbor Motor Inn (now the Bar Harbor Inn) would be built on this spot, affording its guests the same pleasurable view the Hardys had so enjoyed from their veranda.

Photo courtesy of the Maine Historic Preservation Commission

BY 1870, BANGOR RESIDENT Alfred Veazie, a Harvard-educated lawyer, had amassed a fortune, having worked his way up from cashier to president in his grandfather's local bank. Veazie and his wife, Etta (née Hodsdon), bought land from Tobias Roberts and hired Boston's prestigious Doane contracting firm to build their cottage just west of the Hardy place on the shore. The Veazie cottage, now called The Kedge, reflected the post–Civil War preference for the French mansard-style roof, with its distinctive dormered roofline and a picturesque cupola.

After Veazie's death in 1879, the cottage became the home for the Oasis Club, a gentlemen's social group. The house was later moved to West Street and converted back to a summer cottage, which it remains today.

Photo courtesy of the Maine Historic Preservation Commission

THE HIGGINS FAMILY had long ago harvested the trees on this land, creating open pastures for their sheep and a few cows, and were beginning to divide up their property by the time this photograph was taken in the mid-1870s. They sold some of their lots to Bostonians and built rental cottages on others. The foreground area, known as Albert Meadow, was named after its owner, Albert F. Higgins, while the farther section, owned by shipbuilder Stephen Higgins, was called the Field.

In 1869, Harry A. Grant built his stylish Victorian cottage (at right), which later became Grant Park. Next door, fellow Bostonians George R. Minot and his friend F. M. Weld built a pair of plain, unadorned cottages that would eventually be replaced by the Bar Harbor Inn. Albert Higgins built the two cottages on the left to rent out during the summer months.

HENRY MELLEN PRENTISS of Bangor, a Harvard-educated lawyer, wrote extensively on science, especially Arctic exploration. After his lawyer and lumber baron father's death in 1873, Henry took over management of the family's Bangor estate and also hired Bangor architect George W. Orff to build this elaborate seaside residence overlooking Compass Harbor. Orff designed a classic example of an 1870s Stick-style residence, with its wooden decorations on the gables and fanciful bracketing.

Five years later, Edward Coles of Philadelphia purchased the cottage, Aldersea, for $15,000, and added a servants' dining room, laundry and storage rooms, and three bedrooms, the first of several expansions. Aldersea was demolished in the 1960s and replaced by a smaller cottage.

Photo courtesy of the Maine Historic Preservation Commission

ON CHILLY DAYS the Prentiss family could retreat to this "living hall," a functional room that replaced the formal entrance hallway of pre–Civil War era homes. Here the family could enjoy the warmth of a fire as music from the pianoforte (at right) filled the air. This photograph reveals the Prentiss family's eclectic decor. The comfortable lounge chair and a mantelpiece designed to display bric-a-brac illustrate the Eastlake style, which was becoming popular in the 1870s. Fussy Victorian lighting, fringed table linens, and a tall antique case clock on the stair landing complete the diverse nature of this interior. The Indian-motif curtain, a portiere, could be pulled across the room to hold the fire's warmth.

Photo courtesy of the Maine Historic Preservation Commission

WHEN GOUVERNEUR MORRIS OGDEN, son of an eminent New York lawyer who had argued cases before the U.S. Supreme Court, sought to escape from the stench and heat of New York summers, he selected New York architect Charles Coolidge Haight to create this eclectic Stick-style design with mansard rooflines at the middle and end.

Haight's experimentation with the Stick style for Ogden's Watersmeet led to more formal designs for the homes for other members of the New York elite, and, eventually, to his work for Yale University, where he popularized the Gothic Revival style.

After Ogden died in 1880, his family continued to summer in Bar Harbor even after selling Watersmeet to another notable New Yorker, George Washington Vanderbilt.

Photo courtesy of the Bar Harbor Historical Society

MRS. DAVID B. OGDEN, daughter-in-law of Gouverneur Morris Ogden, stands by a rustic settee that exemplifies the Adirondack style. Mrs. Ogden's stylish white dress, with its simplistic cutwork lace neckline, shows the refined fashion popular at the turn of the twentieth century, even as it contrasts with the rustic outdoor furniture in vogue at the same time. The furniture was not built for comfort; rather, it was meant to blend in with the landscape.

Photo courtesy of the Bar Harbor Historical Society

IT'S NO WONDER that the name Vanderbilt is synonymous with the Gilded Age. Members of the family built The Breakers and Marble House in Newport, Elm Court in Lenox, and Shelburne Farms in Vermont.

George Vanderbilt, a twenty-five-year-old bachelor, purchased Pointe d'Acadie (formerly Watersmeet) for his summer home—a quite modest property when compared to his siblings' grand palaces. He brought in Philadelphia architect DeGrasse Fox to expand the space for entertaining and to formalize the landscaping. Fox produced a more fashionable Shingle-style cottage with multiple gabled bays and an overall symmetry. Later, Vanderbilt would hire Central Park landscape architect Frederick Law Olmsted to renovate the grounds.

Although Pointe d'Acadie was a humble retreat on the Vanderbilt scale, George's other project, undertaken simultaneously, was not. Biltmore, his estate in Asheville, North Carolina, would dwarf even his siblings' homes, becoming the largest private residence in the nation.

After George married Edith Stuyvesant (Dresser) in 1898, they expanded Pointe d'Acadie further, and spent most summers there with their daughter, Cornelia, until George's death in 1914. The house changed hands once more, in 1922, to George McFadden, before it was demolished in 1956. What was once a grand estate was later divided into three smaller lots for more modest cottages.

Photo courtesy of the Bar Harbor Historical Society

BOSTONIAN CHARLES F. DORR hired Boston architect Henry Richards to design this elaborate Queen Anne–style cottage, Old Farm. It's impossible to feel bored when looking at this summer home, with its eclectic assortment of materials and surfaces, wide variety of dormers and bays, multiple rooflines, and many balconies. The first-floor exterior stone was quarried from a nearby gorge and is accented by redwood shingles and brick.

Son George B. Dorr grew up in this cottage, set just above Compass Harbor, and later became known as the father of Acadia National Park. According to George Dorr, the seeds for that vision were planted right here at Old Farm: "It was the wonderful beauty of the flowers that grew so naturally and simply in my mother's garden by the sea at Old Farm that, more than aught else, led me along the way, step by step . . . to the founding of Acadia National Park."[2]

Photo courtesy of the Maine Historic Preservation Commission

A BAR HARBOR BARBER once described George Bucknam Dorr, at left in photo, as "looking like a forest." Dorr, the Park's first superintendent, would probably have considered this a compliment. The quiet, affable man, shown here with the Stimsons, loved the island's forests and worked tirelessly in the early 1900s to preserve the mountains and wooded lands for the enjoyment of future generations. With his persistence and personal fortune, he convinced Congress to place the lands in a private trust and convert them to a park. The first success came in 1916, with the designation of Sieur de Monts National Monument, which three years later became Lafayette National Park. At one appropriations committee meeting in the 1920s, a congressman complained that the Maine waters were too cold. Dorr replied, "Sir, I swim every day until Christmas!" This turned the decision in Dorr's favor.[3]

Though the cottage no longer stands, its ruins are now part of Acadia National Park.

Photo courtesy of the Bar Harbor Historical Society

OF THE FORTY-SIX HOUSES that Boston architect William R. Emerson designed in Maine, Redwood is probably the most famous. This was his first cottage in Bar Harbor, designed in 1879 for fellow Bostonian Charles J. Morrill. At Redwood, Emerson created a true example of Shingle style, a design featuring an eclectic combination of rooflines, materials, and exterior ornamentation, and an open interior plan. Shingle style represented a dramatic departure from the traditional rectangular, symmetrical box house with a central front door. Instead of a clapboard exterior, Redwood was sheathed in redwood shingles from the roof down to the foundation.

Redwood remains a summer residence, a tribute to that once-fashionable style.

Photo courtesy of the Bar Harbor Historical Society

FOR HIS THIRD Bar Harbor cottage design, Emerson used varied cuts and patterns of shingles with decorative trim to give a whimsical, playful effect. For the owners of Edgemere, Thomas B. and Fannie Musgrave of New York, it was a place to host dances and musicales. A newspaper account describes a grand ball held there in 1884: "[T]he house [is] all decorated with Japanese lanterns, fans and flowers with colored lights [among] the trees and shrubs. A tent at the entrance for the Bar Harbor band left the whole floor free for dancing . . ."[4] The Musgraves hosted similar entertainments at their Fifth Avenue mansion, no doubt with many of Mr. Musgrave's brokerage clients in attendance.

By 1895, fifteen years after Edgemere's construction, the couple had built two more cottages on their Maine property: Mare Vista, and the larger Eden Hall. In the late 1880s, Thomas faded from the Bar Harbor scene as his business and health failed, but Fannie and their son Percy, a noted Boston surgeon, would live on to enjoy their three cottages.

Photo courtesy of the Maine Historic Preservation Commission

In 1881, William Emerson continued his playful theme, but in a purer Shingle-style form, for Thirlstane, a cottage he designed for Mrs. Rebecca R. Scott of Washington, D.C. In this picturesque structure Emerson incorporated vernacular architectural forms used in New England, such as a saltbox roof.

The second owners, Colonel and Mrs. Edward Morrell, transformed Thirlstane, with assistance from Philadelphia architects, Cope and Stewardson, into a cottage for entertaining. According to the August 19, 1916, *Bar Harbor Life* newspaper, "Col. Morrell's keen sense of humor enabled him to get enjoyment where others would be bored . . . ," and as such, he was the center of most social functions, especially the horse show, which he helped establish.

A love of horses would also be a characteristic of Thirlstane's final owner, William Pierson Hamilton, and his second wife, Theodosia.

Photo courtesy of Raymond Strout

By the 1890s, promenading along the Shore Path had become a fashionable pastime for society ladies and gents, and there was no better vantage point from which to view those strolling by and eavesdrop on the gossip than from the Musgrave Tea Tower. One could enjoy a cup of tea in the second-floor room of this miniature fortress, which measured eighteen feet in diameter. A fireplace warmed visitors on chilly afternoons.

For more active entertainment, Thomas Musgrave built a long, one-story dance hall and bowling alley attached to the tower. Constructed in sections, the one-lane alley could be disassembled to open up the entire eighty-by-eighteen-foot space for dancing.

Photo courtesy of the Maine Historic Preservation Commission

THE DASHING WILLIAM P. HAMILTON, grandson of Alexander Hamilton and former son-in-law and partner to John Pierpont Morgan, whirled into Bar Harbor in 1926. Over a short period he purchased more than 1,500 acres on the island and set out to establish nine ranches featuring state-of-the-art farming practices. His farms housed the finest Belgian mares and stallions, prized Guernsey and Angus cattle, and a superior selection of poultry and sheep. His signature red barns (some of them still visible beside Route 3 north of Bar Harbor) were models of efficiency, and he hired a large professional staff to construct, operate, and maintain them.

At one point in the 1930s, Hamilton was the largest employer in Bar Harbor, and during the Depression era, locals were thankful for the work. Many of his caretakers, gardeners, farmhands, valets, and housekeepers remembered the siestas all employees were required to take, signaled by an alarm that sounded at 1:00 p.m. sharp. By the 1950s, most of his lands had been sold.

Photo courtesy of the Bar Harbor Historical Society

BOSTON ARCHITECTS Rotch and Tilden designed this Queen Anne–style cottage, their first major commission in Bar Harbor, for the widowed Mrs. George Pendleton Bowler of Cincinnati. Extensive trim decorated the half-stone, half-timbered edifice accented by tall towers. In addition to the main house, the grounds included servants' quarters, a caretaker/gardener's cottage, a stable, and a greenhouse. Mrs. Bowler built the twenty-six-bedroom cottage in 1882, and with her two sons, Robert and George, participated in the flurry of Bar Harbor social life. Years later, she sold the estate adjacent to Bear Brook to fellow Midwesterner Joseph P. Pulitzer, the noted press magnate.

Photo courtesy of the Maine Historic Preservation Commission

THE STRESS OF OVERSEEING the daily production of his two newspapers, the *St. Louis Dispatch* and the *New York World*, had affected Joseph Pulitzer's health. Advised by his doctors to rest, the brilliant publisher bought Chatwold in 1894 and hired the eminent New York architectural firm of McKim, Mead, and White to transform the estate into a Normandy-like village. Their design reflected the European style then becoming part of the Gilded Age trend.

At left, the forty-foot-square Tower of Silence dominated the edifice. Inside the three-story stone tower, Pulitzer could swim in the heated pool (a novelty in Bar Harbor), study, dine, and sleep—all the time being completely insulated from outside noises. Even with all his wealth and influence, however, he could not silence the nearby foghorn on Egg Rock.

Photo courtesy of the Maine Historic Preservation Commission

ALTHOUGH JOSEPH PULITZER craved silence, his wife and children fully participated in the lively Bar Harbor social scene, which included hosting sophisticated dinner parties at Chatwold. Guests would be greeted in this impressive hall. Furnished in the Italian Renaissance style, it featured a grand center table and elaborately carved chairs and chests. No doubt the Pulitzers had gathered the antiques and paintings while touring Europe. An armchair of seventeenth-century Flemish style is visible on the landing in the upper right. An odd note in this baronial interior is the upholstered "Turkish" chair near the window on the left. As Betsy Field, the daughter of caretaker Ralph Field, remembered, "Life there was like a fairy tale."

In contrast to the formality of their summer domicile, the Pulitzer family enjoyed casual activities such as hikes on the surrounding mountains and horseback rides through the woods. For complete relaxation, they would cruise around Frenchman Bay and beyond on their three-hundred-foot yacht *Liberty*.

Photo courtesy of Raymond Strout

For Pulitzer, his wife Kate, and their seven children—Ralph, Lucille, Katherine, Joseph Jr., Edith, Constance, and Herbert—Chatwold and summer were synonymous. They arrived each year with a large staff, including Pulitzer's six secretaries. (Biographer Dan Pfaff asserts that the magnate could wear out all six in a single day.) After Pulitzer died in 1911, Mrs. Pulitzer continued to spend the summers at Chatwold, surrounded by her children and grandchildren.

When Joseph Jr. inherited the estate in 1924, the pattern continued for many years. Hikes, horseback rides, tennis, golf, picnics on surrounding islands, formal dinner parties, and swims and dances at the club filled their days. Joseph Jr. downsized to a more practical, seventy-five-foot schooner for their sails along the coast.

As Joseph III told a family tutor in 1929, "It's nice to have money. I haven't any, but Father has some, and one can have yachts and so forth." Even with their significant fortune, Chatwold's size and operating expense became a burden, and the Pulitzers had the house demolished in 1946—ironically, just a year before the 1947 fire burned across the property.

Photo courtesy of the Maine Historic Preservation Commission

The Rawle and Jones families, members of Philadelphia's fashionable society, had long summered in Newport. By the 1880s, however, sophisticated social rituals were replacing the informal atmosphere there, which led Frederick Jones, his wife, Mary Cadwalader Rawle, and daughter Beatrix, to visit Bar Harbor instead. Jones's sister, society novelist Edith Wharton, visited as well, and found that she preferred the village's active lifestyle and the intellectual conversation to Newport's.

By 1883, the now-divorced Mary Jones hired Rotch and Tilden to design this six-bedroom cottage, Reef Point, on the shore path. The stark, snowy background of this photo accentuates the architect's simple design.

For the young Beatrix Jones (later Farrand), shown standing in front of the cottage in 1886, Reef Point became her canvas each summer as she experimented with the art of landscaping.

Photo courtesy of the Environmental Design Archives, The University of California at Berkeley

LOCAL RESIDENT GEORGE HIGGINS built this house as a summer rental. This photo shows guests departing on a buckboard excursion soon after Joseph P. Bass and his wife Mary, (née March), purchased the house from Higgins in 1893. Bass was the owner and publisher of the *Bangor Commercial* newspaper for forty years and was active in civil affairs at both the state and local levels. He made renovations to the cottage, which was located in the Field up the hill from Hardy's cottage (pages 55 and 56). In 1932, Mrs. Ana Murch and Mrs. Fred Moore purchased it for $15,000. Today, as an inn, it still provides vacationers with a comfortable place to stay.

Photo courtesy of the Bar Harbor Historical Society

OVER THE YEARS, Mary Jones expanded Reef Point both inside and out. To accommodate her visiting friends and family, she hired local architect John Clark to expand the outdoor living spaces by adding balconies and terraces.

The surrounding landscape showcased daughter Beatrix's talent as a landscape designer. She had apprenticed with Bostonian Charles Sprague Sargent, director of the Arnold Arboretum, and what had begun as a pastime developed into a full-time profession. By the time she married Yale professor Max Farrand in 1913, Beatrix had started work on the Princeton University campus. That commission led to others from the J. P. Morgan Library in New York, Acadia National Park, and Dumbarton Oaks in Washington, D.C., whose gardens became her masterpiece.

Later, in 1939, Beatrix and her husband, Max, developed their Reef Point property as a botanical garden, a learning center for horticulturalists, both professional and amateur. In the 1950s, perceiving a lack of long-term support to continue the center once she was gone, Beatrix dismantled the gardens and razed the cottage.

Photo courtesy of the Maine Historic Preservation Commission

In 1884, Alpheus and Susan Hardy hired Boston architects Charles Cummings and Willard T. Sears, famous for the New Old South Church design, to create a more elaborate cottage than Birch Point. Their resulting classic Queen Anne design featured roughly hewn granite, with red grout on the ground floor, extensive half-timbering on the second story, and a multi-gabled roof. The Hardys built this cottage, Ullikana, intending to lease it, but after Mr. Hardy's death in 1887, Mrs. Hardy and her four sons used it themselves during the summers.

The cottage's name comes from a Hawaiian tale about a horse that becomes a savior to other island horses, in much the same way that Alpheus Hardy had mentored several young men. Not only had he become the guardian to Montgomery Sears, whom he raised as a son, he also sponsored a young Japanese boy named Neesima Shimeta, who became a missionary pastor and established Japan's first Christian college, Doshisha University, in Kyoto.

Photo courtesy of the Maine Historic Preservation Commission

As one of the most prominent politicians of post–Civil War America, running unsuccessfully for president in 1884 and serving three presidents as secretary of state, James G. Blaine was conscious of his role in both politics and society. He selected architect William Masters Camac, a partner with the Philadelphia firm of Furness, Evans and Co., to design his summer home. Camac, a longtime Bar Harbor summer resident himself, created a fanciful interpretation of the Queen Anne style, as shown in this oceanside view of Stanwood. He pushed the style to the edge with oversized gables and a variety of materials and forms, creating a distinctive cottage for Blaine and his family.

After Blaine's death, his wife and surviving children— James G. Blaine Jr., Robert S. Blaine, Harriet Blaine Beale, and Margaret Blaine Damrosch, wife of composer Walter Damrosch—continued to summer at Stanwood and entertain nationally prominent figures there.

Photo courtesy of the Maine Historic Preservation Commission

Harriet Stanwood Blaine is credited with helping her husband to attain his national political stature. She managed all the social aspects of Blaine's political career, including President Harrison's six-day sojourn at their Bar Harbor cottage in early August 1889. Bar Harbor society rolled out the red carpet for his visit with a flurry of receptions. During a pause in the social schedule, a group gathered on Stanwood's vast veranda to record this historic event. From left are President Harrison, Mrs. James Blaine and her husband, Mrs. Henry Cabot Lodge and her husband, Secretary to the President E. W. Halford, possibly Margaret Blaine, Walker Blaine, and James Blaine Jr.

The attendance list read like a Who's Who of American society, including Maine senator Eugene Hale, author Mrs. Burton Harrison, the Aulick Palmers of Chicago, George Vanderbilt, Bostonian Morris K. Jesup, lawyer David B. Ogden, and the foreign ministers of France, Turkey, and Italy.

Photo courtesy of the Maine Historic Preservation Commission

ALBERT C. BARNEY was delighted with the newspaper headlines that highlighted his new Bar Harbor summer cottage, Ban-y-Bryn, his castle in both design and name. Soon after inheriting a $5 million fortune, built on railway car manufacturing, Barney began a building spree, commissioning New York architects Stratton and Quimby to create this twenty-six-room fortress while at the same time financing a palatial estate in Washington, D.C. Completed in 1889, Stratton's design of massive masonry and stucco in a Romanesque Revival style demonstrated Albert's pursuit of social stature.

His wife, Ohio heiress Alice Pike, was a noted painter, and for her the residence provided a venue to nurture the arts. She and her three daughters hosted teas and musicales there. At one such occasion, daughter Natalie and her friends, dressed in colorful Spanish garb topped with mantillas, amused more than two hundred prominent socialites with an assortment of dances.

This Norman Road castle, later owned by Joseph Wholean, burned in the 1947 fire.

Photo courtesy of Raymond Strout

ALICE BARNEY stands at the entrance to one of the many balconies of her new residence. For this area, Mrs. Barney selected a suite of heavy bamboo furniture that effectively evoked the outdoors, combined with a fine Persian carpet to add a note of refinement to the space. "No expense has been spared to make it [Ban-y-Bryn] a most elegant and comfortable residence," reported the May 2, 1889, *Bar Harbor Record*. Mr. George Barron, the contractor for the project, commented that the cottage exhibited some of the finest-quality woodwork in all of Bar Harbor, including carved solid oak railings, balusters, and newel posts ornamented with papier-mâché. Suggesting the style of a medieval baronial castle, the living room's seven-foot-deep fireplace protruded into the room to allow seating all around. Over the front rested an immense eight-inch-thick, nine-foot-long granite mantel. With the castle complete, the lord and lady were ready to entertain.

Photo courtesy of the Smithsonian Institution Archives[5]

ALTHOUGH NEW YORKERS represented the highest number of cottage owners, followed by Bostonians and then Philadelphians, the Midwesterners gradually gained in numbers and prominence. By the time of this photo (c. 1889), Bar Harbor had become popular with Cincinnati's society families.

One summer day, the Barney family went to visit their fellow Cincinnatians, the Pendletons, who owned two cottages—the Barnacles (shown here), and Bagatelle—nearby. While Albert Barney and his daughter Laura rode on horseback down the hill from Ban-y-Bryn, Alice and her daughter Natalie, shown standing on the porch, preferred to drive in their elegant carriage.

Lawyer Edmund Pendleton needed ample room for visits from his extended family, which included his siblings: George, an Ohio senator and minister to Germany; Elliott, president of the Kentucky Central Railroad; and Charlotte, a Philadelphia education reformer—all prominent members of society. Mrs. Robert Bowler, stepsister to Edmund, lived nearby at her Chatwold estate.

Photo courtesy of the Smithsonian Institution Archives[6]

NEW YORK ARCHITECTS Rowe and Baker designed Kenarden Lodge in an eclectic style that combined French chateauesque turrets with English half-timbered features. Scotsman and New York banker John Stewart Kennedy and his wife, Emma (née Baker), built the estate in 1892, spending more than $200,000 ($23 million in today's dollars).

The childless couple was popular in the Bar Harbor social network. Kennedy was known for his cheery disposition, amply matched by his wife's playful personality and good business sense. Both were dedicated to local and New York charities. Before his death in 1909, Kennedy gave liberally to the library and the Village Improvement Society, and donated land that would later become part of Acadia National Park. Mrs. Kennedy's imprint on the village can also be seen today. She was the prime benefactor for the local hospital, the YWCA building on Mount Desert Street, and the Y Athletic Field.

Photo courtesy of the Maine Historic Preservation Commission

COTTAGE AT BAR HARBOR ME. 174,

YACHTSMEN SAILING around Bald Porcupine Island around 1910 would have seen this view of Kenarden Lodge. Newspaper accounts of the day describe the house at night as a "fairy palace" with its hundreds of incandescent lights. It did help to have an electric plant on-site!

After Mrs. Kennedy's death in 1929, the John T. Dorrance family of Radnor, Pennsylvania, became the second owners. Dorrance, a European-trained chemist, had invented condensed soup in 1897, enabling the Campbell Company to reduce can sizes and broaden its product line while saving money. As the company's profits rose, so too did Dorrance's.

Despite the Depression, the Dorrances maintained Kenarden's charm. One "entered by a long drive beside a wooded brook, suddenly opening out to wide lawns, old trees and bright colored flower beds." The succeeding generation chose a simpler lifestyle and replaced the expansive granite residence with a smaller cottage in the 1970s.

Photo courtesy of the Maine Historic Preservation Commission

THIS ITALIAN GARDEN at Kenarden Lodge was primarily a "green garden," featuring a pergola executed with classical features, masonry walls draped with foliage to enclose the setting, a central fountain, and large terra-cotta pots strategically placed around the grounds. It was sited with Newport Mountain as a distant prospect. This more formal garden style was increasingly becoming the standard for cottages in Bar Harbor by the 1890s, demonstrating the owner's social status. Though Mrs. Kennedy held many garden parties for the elite at Kenarden, she also welcomed the public to come and take a stroll within its romantic enclave one Sunday a month.

Photo courtesy of the Maine Historic Preservation Commission

IT WAS NO COINCIDENCE that Kenarden entertainments could offer sumptuous grapes and delicate greens in rooms exploding with floral colors. In the last years of the nineteenth and into the twentieth centuries, "grape houses" became popular in the United States and Scotland, enabling owners to enjoy the fruit earlier in the season. Mrs. Kennedy's gardens were well known, as were her greenhouses, overseen for many years by superintendent William T. Burton (with tie). Both the Kennedys, and, later, the Dorrances, could dine on sweet oranges, luscious, plump grapes, and an assortment of fresh produce. Tubbed and potted plants were grown in the greenhouse to transform Kenarden's interior rooms and porches into tropical havens. During the winter, some estate greenhouses continued to grow produce that was shipped to the cottager's winter residence.

Photo courtesy of the Bar Harbor Historical Society

WITH THE COMPLETION of Reverie Cove in 1893, Bar Harbor architecture entered a new phase with the Classical Revival style. The Victorian picturesque method, with its storybook turrets and eclectic features, gave way to a symmetrical design using elements of the Beaux Arts and Colonial Revival styles: square-pillared porches, a low-pitched roof, and arched windows. The soft yellow stucco exterior highlighted the clean architectural features.

This was local architect Fred L. Savage's first major commission in Bar Harbor. A Northeast Harbor native, Savage apprenticed with the Boston firm of Peabody and Stearns, and six years later designed this "Spanish"-style villa for Mr. and Mrs. John Davies Jones of Washington, D.C. Jones, a noted international agriculturalist, his wife, and daughter Martina, the future Marchese Lanza d'Ajeta, would only stay a decade in Bar Harbor before selling to Mrs. Abram Hewitt, widow of the steel magnate and New York City mayor Abram S. Hewitt.

Photo courtesy of the Maine Historic Preservation Commission

CONTINUING THE Colonial Revival style, Savage designed the first floor to facilitate entertaining with this dining room and its opposite square parlor flanking the expansive central living hall. The woodwork, originally stained in a dark Flemish oak, emphasized the formal decor carried out with the Hepplewhite-style sideboard, a tall case clock with elegant inlaid decorations, brocade-paneled walls, and an ornamental "Adamesque" mantelpiece with delicate garlands and scrolls. Despite the formality of the villa's furnishings, the parties at Reverie Cove were alive with dancing and fun, especially under Mrs. Hewitt's reign with her family tribe of three daughters and three sons.

Industrialist DeForest Grant preserved the house through the tumultuous mid-twentieth century, and it remains a private home today, listed in the National Register of Historic Places.

Photo courtesy of the Maine Historic Preservation Commission

By 1900, Robert Hall McCormick, son of the reaping machine inventor, could look out from his Asian arched window at the estates of his fellow Midwestern millionaires. He probably knew neighbor Walter S. Gurnee, a former Chicago mayor, called "the Father of the North Shore." William R. Emerson, the Boston architect, designed the three-story residence at the far left for Gurnee in 1882. Chicago architect Daniel Burnham created another Shingle-style cottage (shown at right) for St. Louis industrialist John Whittaker and his wife, Violet. Another industrialist and Cincinnati real estate baron named John J. Emery completed the Midwestern triumvirate when he built the chateau called the Turrets, with its gatehouse in front, as a wedding present for his new bride, Lela Alexander. In a few short years, Emery wanted to expand his estate, and did so by replacing the former Whittaker residence, the Moorings, with gardens.

Photo courtesy of the Bar Harbor Historical Society

In 1893, just after completing the grand Château Frontenac Hotel in Old Quebec City, New York architect Bruce Price began to design this smaller-scale residence for John Emery. Price's entry into Bar Harbor architecture had occurred fifteen years prior with the West End Hotel. After that, wealthy families called upon him to design mansions in Tuxedo Park, Newport, and other elite resorts.

Not only does this cottage's size offer the feeling of a fortress, but its native granite facade, quarried on Mount Desert Island near Eagle Lake, also emphasizes its mass. It took two years—and $100,000—for contractor John Clark, mason Calvin Norris, and a full crew to build the Turrets. Impressed by the results, Emery hired Clark to design additions in later years.

Photo courtesy of the Maine Historic Preservation Commission

THE FOYER OF THE TURRETS, designed in a Classical Revival style, befit the lavish entertainments hosted by Lela and John Emery. As guests entered, they could admire the heavily carved neo-Renaissance furniture: the hall table at right, supported with carved griffins; the oversized chair with a cushion for weary feet; and an ornate cupboard used to display Oriental vases, probably collected during the family's world travels.

It may have been on one of these trips that Lela Emery met British aristocrat Alfred Anson after her husband's death in 1908. The couple married in 1912 and continued summering at the Turrets with her five children. Lord Anson probably felt quite comfortable surrounded by European antiques.

Years later, the Turrets would pass through several owners, and for a while housed a seminary for the Franco-American Oblate Fathers, before being restored by the College of the Atlantic in the 1970s.

Photo courtesy of the Maine Historic Preservation Commission

LOCATED TO THE SOUTH of the Turrets was this four-thousand-square-foot sunken garden, noted by some as the first hanging garden in Bar Harbor. Towering blue delphinium defined the edge of the garden in the foreground. This woman in the photo, thought to be Alexandra, daughter of J. J. Emery, is shown here collecting blooms, which suggests that this was both an ornamental and a cutting garden.

Large terra-cotta pots were used to draw the eye to different parts of the garden. The ones in this photograph marked the garden's north entrance. A pair of Lombardy poplars near the house adds to the ambience of seclusion. Remnants of this garden can be found today behind the College of the Atlantic administration building, formerly the Turrets.

Photo courtesy of the Jesup Memorial Library

HAVING SUMMERED at Schooner Head in Bar Harbor, architect Herbert Jaques understood Mrs. Carpenter's desire for a fashionable look. By replacing Edenfield's heavy mansard roof with a multi-gabled third floor, Jaques and his firm lightened the residence's appearance. To achieve this feat, masons and carpenters covered part of the original stone exterior with half-timbered decorations, as shown in this photo.

Inside this cottage, newly renamed Hauterive, Mrs. Carpenter's appreciation of the French and Italian masters was evident in both name and design.

Her great-niece described the combination of styles: "[T]he delicately and lightly decorated drawing room furnished in the French eighteenth-century style by Duveen" greeted guests as they entered the front hall. In the dining room, the red-lacquer furniture, suggested by Baron de Meyer, stood in stark contrast to the soft greenish-gray carpet. Shelves were filled with books on Pre-Raphaelite art, "making a quiet cultured corner of American life strongly influenced by Pre-Raphaelism," according to her great-niece.

Photo courtesy of the Bar Harbor Historical Society

EDENFIELD, a modest cottage along Eden Street, combined two floors of solid granite with an overbearing mansard roof. There was no doubt that Mrs. Miles B. Carpenter, a New York widow known for her fashionable, sophisticated tastes, would renovate this residence after she purchased it from the Samuel Lyons estate for about $75,000 in October 1898. With her daughter Agnes by her side, Josephine Carpenter hired the Andrews, Jaques, and Rantoul firm to extensively alter the cottage.

Photo courtesy of the Bar Harbor Historical Society

IT WAS OBVIOUS from the architectural plans for Hauterive that Josephine and Agnes Carpenter enjoyed the outdoors. The small porches of the original structure were replaced with a broad terrace along the entire length of the house, affording a sitting area outside the drawing room and an eating area outside the dining room. Flowers planted in large pottery jars at the edge of the terrace attracted hummingbirds and butterflies.

This photograph shows the cottage garden that separated the terrace and a lawn that sloped down to the semicircular balustrade above the bay. The plentiful outdoor venues offered an assortment of activities: marble seats to view passing boats, a croquet lawn for refined matches, and a rose garden with a maze of brick paths ending at a fountain—a perfect spot for afternoon tea.

Photo courtesy of the Bar Harbor Historical Society

MODELING THEIR NEW Paris acquisitions, Josephine (left) and Agnes Carpenter (right) were prepared for the summer's festivities. Annually the two would travel overseas, shopping in Paris for the newest fashions and pampering themselves in the curative waters of Karlsbad, "returning to Hauterive in June for the summer and to the life of comfort and luxury of a past era," recalled her great-niece.

Agnes, a noted lover of the outdoors, enjoyed Bar Harbor to such an extent that one year she stayed until Thanksgiving, driving her staff mad with alternating bouts of bursting pipes and boredom. Agnes passed away after ninety years of summering (not wintering) at Hauterive with her nieces, nephews, and friends.

Although the estate escaped the 1947 fire, it was later replaced by the Regency Hotel (now known as the Bar Harbor Regency).

Photo courtesy of the Bar Harbor Historical Society

ABOUT THE TIME of the great stock market crash of 1929, local mason John Preble and his crew began working on the Hauterive garden, giving it a modern transformation. They replaced the romantic, delicate English rose garden with one featuring hardscape: a fifteen-foot-high red granite wall in the shape of a half-moon, surrounding a double fountain structure. An immense, ten-ton slab of granite formed a platform in front of the fountain area. Contractors transported this enormous flat rock across the bay by boat and then used a system of shims and rollers to maneuver it into place.

Contrasting with this informal style were the antique statues perched on the ends of the half-moon wall and a picturesque European fountain in the center. When the new, secluded garden was completed, Agnes Carpenter and her guests could enjoy the cool summer breezes, shaded by stately trees.

Photo courtesy of the Bar Harbor Historical Society

PIPE IN HAND, Eric Ellis Soderholtz is seated, surrounded by the sturdy
garden vases he designed for estates all along the East Coast, but especially on
Mount Desert Island. The Swedish-born architectural photographer began
his American journey in Boston, working for the Museum of Fine Arts. While
spending summers in his wife's hometown of West Gouldsboro, Maine,
he became frustrated attempting to garden in the rocky soil. To resolve the
problem, Soderholtz began producing concrete garden containers that would
withstand Maine's frigid winter temperatures. His pieces, inspired by the
Mediterranean pots he had photographed in his earlier days, caught the eye of
Beatrix Farrand, who began incorporating them into her landscape designs.
Soon his urns, birdbaths, vases, and fountains could be found in formal gardens
across the eastern seaboard, including at Hauterive. Some of his creations, such
as the winged fountain gracing Bar Harbor's Agamont Park, continue to lure
visitors who try to catch its spray.

Photo courtesy of Raymond Strout

AT THE DAWN of the twentieth century, George S. Bowdoin, Esq.,
a J. P. Morgan financier and philanthropist, joined the Bar Harbor summer
colony by building La Rochelle near the intersection of West and Eden
streets. Reflecting the Huguenot heritage of Mrs. Julia (Grinnell) Bowdoin,
architects Andrews, Jaques and Rantoul created a chateau-influenced style
for the Bowdoin cottage. Architectural writer I. Howland Jones noted that
the "native water-struck brick of a beautiful texture and great variety of
color, enlivened by warm buff limestone trimmings," offered a soft effect to
the broad residence.

Over the years, the estate owners, including Tristram Colket, son
of Kenarden's John Dorrance, expanded the estate to include houses for
the caretakers and the chauffeur, a carpenter's shop with a lathe forge, a
dedicated heating plant, and three greenhouses. Later in the century La
Rochelle became home to the Maine Sea Coast Mission, bringing care and
ministry to isolated residents on Maine's outer islands.

Photo courtesy of the Maine Historic Preservation Commission

"AVAMAYA" — RESIDENCE OF MAJOR WHEELER.

FROM AVAMAYA, his cottage perched at the brow of Highbrook Road, Major George Wheeler of the Army Corps of Engineers enjoyed a panoramic view of the bay, Bar Harbor village, and Cadillac Mountain. New York architect Sidney Stratton and his associate Frank Quimby designed this original stone and half-timbered residence in 1888, using unstained shingles on the upper floors and reddish granite on the lower stories. Successive owners in the following two decades made additions using designs by local architect Fred Savage.

With its multiple partial turrets and verandas, Avamaya exuded the fanciful air of an Eastern Continental castle. Stratton continued this theme inside, with an elliptical-shaped parlor and another room that featured a rough-cast wall surface above the wainscoting. Unusual shapes and materials were becoming commonplace for local contractors like Avamaya's George Barron, who were being tested with each new design, innovation, and style that caught the fancy of their wealthy clients.

Photo courtesy of the Maine Historic Preservation Commission

AROUND 1901, noted lawyer DeWitt Clinton Blair of New Jersey, president of Belvidere Bank, and his wife Mary Ann Kimball purchased the Avamaya estate. Though they appreciated the cottage's turrets, dormers, and vertical emphasis, they hired architects Andrews, Jaques, and Rantoul to polish it into a more stately residence with correspondingly elegant grounds.

Local contractor A. E. Lawrence assembled this massive crew to carry out the new grounds plan, cutting two drives into the steep grade that wound sinuously up to the entrance. Architectural writer I. Howland Jones noted that in order to soften the retaining walls lining the drives, the masons used long granite blocks specially cut to emphasize their horizontal planes.

Lawrence also called upon his crew to transplant fifty-foot trees from nearby forests to grace the area around the residence. Jones reported that this process amused the local lumbermen doing the work, who referred to it as "[fulfilling] the whims of the city people."[7]

Photo courtesy of the Raymond Strout

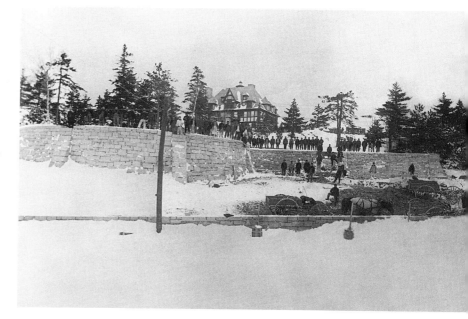

WITH THE RENOVATIONS complete, the Blair family renamed the estate Blair Eyrie and moved in during the spring of 1902, with the whole family in tow, including sons C. Ledyard and John Insley Blair and their wives and children. The Blair name already graced Blairstown, New Jersey, Blair Hall at Princeton, and Blair & Co. on Wall Street, so the name change was not a surprise.

Son Ledyard Blair was involved with the legendary *Kronprinzessin Cecilie*, an ocean liner that became stranded in Bar Harbor at the outbreak of World War I. On a trip across the Atlantic, the elegant liner, carrying more than a thousand people and $14 million in German gold bullion, was ordered to turn back to Europe. Instead, she silently sought refuge along the U.S. coast. It was passenger Ledyard Blair, an experienced yachtsman, who safely piloted the massive ship to Bar Harbor, where she stayed for four months.

Photo courtesy of the Maine Historic Preservation Commission

JUST AS GEORGE BOWDOIN had adopted a French style for the exterior of his cottage, La Rochelle, the Blairs applied this same panache to their formal parlor at Blair Eyrie. In this photo, the room awaits Mrs. Blair's lady friends for tea, when they might chat about the Kebo Valley Club dinner of the previous night, or the whist game scheduled for the following afternoon.

Mrs. Blair selected furniture for this parlor in the French neoclassical style, with a striped wall covering, an elegant chandelier, and a Louis XVI–style settee and armchair. The marble-top table, also of Louis XVI style, was draped with a crewelwork cloth of eighteenth-century design, and topped with a mid-nineteenth-century American lamp. Guests could choose either of the French-style caned bergère chairs seen at left. The room is graced with a fresh bouquet of zinnias, probably just picked from the estate's garden.

Photo courtesy of the Maine Historic Preservation Commission

THE BOLDLY PATTERNED Indian fabrics draped from this sitting room's ceiling and hung on the wall, as well as the Egyptian souvenir tapestries, attest to the turn-of-the-century taste for exoticism, and may reflect the particular travel experiences of the Blair family. Native American baskets echo the circular designs of the oriental fabrics. The Arts and Crafts bureau (at right) and the rocking chair (at left) are combined with wicker and bamboo pieces to make this informal room fun and inviting.

Photo courtesy of the Maine Historic Preservation Commission

Garden at Blair Eyrie.
Bar Harbor, Me.

AT THE HEIGHT of the growing season, this Italian garden was ready for the Blairs' annual reception, when the greater part of Bar Harbor's summer colony would enjoy an afternoon of strolling along the paths and enjoying refreshments in the teahouse just beyond the entrance. From this angle, one can see how Greenleaf situated the garden for a beautiful vista of Champlain Mountain in the distance. Arcs of colorful phlox, lilies, dahlias, and hollyhocks surround the dragon fountain, the central focal point of the garden. These blossoms and shrubs softened the appearance of Maine's proud pines.

Photo courtesy of the Maine Historic Preservation Commission

DESIGNING THE PATHWAYS and garden on the steep slopes below Blair Eyrie posed a challenge for James Greenleaf, recognized as one of the foremost landscape architects during the Country Place era around the turn of the twentieth century. Greenleaf, possibly shown at right, sought to blend the artistry of a formal garden within a circle of Maine white pines by using symmetrical patterns for the planting materials and pathways, enclosing the area with walls and hedges, and gradually building up the height of the plantings from the center to the edges. In this picture, one can see the outlines of the beds and paths for this rectangular area, which measured one hundred feet by two hundred feet in size.

Photo courtesy of Raymond Strout

ALTHOUGH CLASSIFIED as Italianate, the garden at Blair Eyrie also featured Asian design elements, including this Japanese fountain and a quaint shingled teahouse draped with vines. The cast bronze dragon, surrounded by a pool where glistening orange goldfish swam, introduced playfulness to the atmosphere as water flowed from the dragon's mouth.

By the 1900s, water played an important role in garden design, not only because of its innate popularity as a garden feature, but also due to advances in engineering. The combination of sweet, blossom-scented air and the sound of trickling water created a mesmerizing mood for the garden visitor.

In 1935, the Blair family tore down the estate, which eventually became the site for the current-day Summit House Health Care Center.

Photo courtesy of the Maine Historic Preservation Commission

As the daughter of John Dustin Archbold, long-standing Standard Oil Company president and leader, Anne Archbold studied and traveled all over the world. During those adventures, the heiress and artist collected specific ideas for a cottage in Bar Harbor. In her travels to Europe she collected photographs of Italian villas and compiled them into a miniature model. At the age of thirty, she commissioned Bar Harbor architect Fred Savage to supervise the building of her oasis. When completed in 1904, the bold square tower of the Florentine-style villa rose out of the Eden Heights hills, surrounded by pointed firs. This commission was probably one of Savage's most exotic.

Photo courtesy of the Bar Harbor Historical Society

Leopard skins draped on a wicker chaise add an exotic note to this dining room, where "Jacobean" Revival chairs are combined with China Trade plant stands. As was common in the West, a Chinese porcelain fishbowl (on the left) is being used as a planter.

A talented artist, Anne Archbold was also known as a vivacious and colorful character who enjoyed entertaining a wide variety of guests. Colorful characters have lively stories to tell, but Anne definitely did not want the gossip shared. Ingenuity and engineering solved the problem. The middle of her dining room table, shown at center, could be mechanically lowered to the kitchen below, eliminating the need for sharp-eared servants in the dining room. With this advantage, Anne and her guests could gossip while gazing out of the expansive windows over the foothills of Bar Harbor.

Photo courtesy of the Bar Harbor Historical Society

ANNE ARCHBOLD'S BOUDOIR was as famous for its decor as were any of the rooms surrounding it. The neo-Renaissance armchairs and "Jacobean" Revival furniture with twist-turned legs complemented the virtual altar that Mrs. Archbold had created. The animal skins and Oriental chest illustrate the taste for the exotic that was popular in this period. Adjacent to her boudoir, Mrs. Archbold could relax in her Roman bath, a deep, tiled tub reached by descending several steps. At the corner of her room, a spiral iron staircase led to the tower above. True to an Italian villa design, Savage also included a loggia, or recessed piazza, on the second floor. Though the loggia was enclosed in glass, the windows could be opened, enabling Archbold and her three children, Mary, Moira, and John, to enjoy the breeze on cool summer evenings as they took in the panoramic mountain views. Sadly, the raging flames of the 1947 fire on Mount Desert Island burned Archbold Villa to the ground.

Photo courtesy of the Bar Harbor Historical Society

IN THIS VIEW, evening light casts a long shadow on the Archbolds' Mediterranean-style courtyard with its whimsical fountain. American artist Janet Scudder created this bronze sculpture in 1900, influenced by Italian Renaissance sculptures. In her autobiography, she described its origin: "In that moment a finished work flashed before me. I saw a little boy dancing, laughing, and chuckling all to himself while a spray of water dashed over him. The idea of my Frog Fountain was born."[8]

This work energized Scudder's career. The following year, Scudder joined Archbold on a trip to the Far East as her guest. This friendship may have led to a connection with architect Stanford White, of the New York firm, McKim, Mead and White, who purchased a version of the sculpture and provided her with commissions for several years. Scudder produced only four large copies of this fountain, and it was fitting that one of these found a home in Archbold's Italian villa.

Photo courtesy of Raymond Strout

ALEXANDER J. CASSATT'S LIFE would revolve around railroads. He started as an engineer for the Pennsylvania Railroad, and later served as its president. Brother to the now-famous Impressionist painter Mary Cassatt, Alexander sought a relaxed haven to ease the stress of overseeing the construction of New York's Penn Station and its associated railroad tunnels. He hired Horace S. Frazer, prominent architect for many Brookline, Massachusetts, homes, to design "a big roomy house . . . yet of modest and quiet design," according to an article in the July 1910 edition of *American Homes and Gardens* magazine.

Frazer achieved this by sticking to simple lines and styles, both inside and out. On the exterior a stucco first floor blended with dark shingles on the second. Terraces and balconies on the shore side offered ample places to take in the ocean's views and refreshing breezes. Throughout the home's public rooms, Mission-style furniture offered comfort without pretentiousness. Gray-green grasscloth, a faddish style of that period, coated the walls in some rooms, and bluish burlap covered others.

Photo courtesy of the Maine Historic Preservation Commission

GRANDMOTHER CASSATT enjoys a relaxing afternoon on the Four Acres porch with her twenty-year-old granddaughter Lois (at right), Lois's future husband, John B. Thayer (at far left), and his brother Theodore. By the 1920s, these families had left this cottage for other destinations. Mrs. Cassatt chose the rival resort in Newport, while Lois and her banker husband sought a quieter summer life, which they found at a small farm in Bar Harbor's neighboring community of Hulls Cove.

John Thayer knew the precious value of life. At age seventeen, he had survived the sinking of the *Titanic*, clinging to an overturned lifeboat overnight before being rescued, along with his mother and brother. He lost his father in that tragedy. As John's daughters would recall, he would come to Maine from his job as financial vice president of the University of Pennsylvania to relax, not to entertain.

Photo courtesy of the Bar Harbor Historical Society

THE CASSATT PROPERTY has a long history of occupation by prominent families. After the Cassatts moved to Hulls Cove, Mr. and Mrs. Frederick Vanderbilt rented the property for several years around World War I. Soon after, Philadelphians Edward T. and Eva Stotesbury purchased the estate. Like Cassatt, Edward Stotesbury was a self-made millionaire, having worked his way up from an office boy at Drexel & Co. to become a senior partner there, and, later, at J. P. Morgan & Co. After his first wife died, he married widow Lucretia (Eva) Roberts Cromwell in 1912. She too had worked her way up, but in her case it was through marriage and into Mrs. Astor's New York social circles. The pair

complemented each other. The dapper, genial Edward liked to make money and the elegant Eva liked to spend it . . . lavishly. In just over a decade, the couple built three palaces: one in Philadelphia, one in Palm Beach, and lastly, Wingwood House, the vastly remodeled Cassatt estate, shown here.

Photo courtesy of the Bar Harbor Historical Society

DURING THE FIRST DECADE the Cassatt family summered in Bar Harbor, this scene would have been impossible. In 1903, the summer colony, grappling for ways to maintain their elegant island excursions, banned noisy, malodorous automobiles from Bar Harbor and its neighboring summer resorts. Despite protests from the year-round residents who spoke up in favor of the practicalities of auto use, the restrictions continued for ten years. It took an act of the Maine Legislature in 1913 to allow vehicles in Bar Harbor. The change drove some cottagers to other resorts, whereas others, like Lois Cassatt Thayer and her husband, John B. Thayer III, immediately adopted the practice themselves. As Edith Wharton commented, the "motor" restored the romance of travel, as this couple shows. By 1925, more than 5,680 cars passed through the corner of Main and Cottage streets in twelve hours—eight cars per minute.

Photo courtesy of the Bar Harbor Historical Society

THIS BAYSIDE VIEW of the completed Wingwood House shows what is viewed as the largest Colonial-style residence ever built in Maine. It evolved over several years, with Eva Stotesbury overseeing every detail. Though Eva was known for her elegant charm, she also micromanaged her projects with exacting standards. The first architect, Palm Beach's Howard Major, was replaced soon after the completion of the main section with Philadelphian Louis Magaziner, a partner in the firm of Magaziner, Eberhard, and Harris. The house grew with each design refinement, until the central section rose up to four floors, each with 11,000 square feet. The challenge for Magaziner was to include all the features Mrs. Stotesbury desired, while still

keeping the entire project in scale. Local contractor E. K. Whitaker not only supervised the project, but also contributed his carpentry skills to some of the home's cabinetry and wood details. Nationally known landscaper and Bar Harbor resident Beatrix Farrand applied her talents to the Wingwood House project, accenting the house with pergolas, terraces, and lawns that sloped gently down to the bay.

Photo courtesy of Maine Historic Preservation Commission

ARCHITECT LOUIS MAGAZINER could hold British art dealer Joseph Duveen responsible for some of his design headaches at Wingwood. In mid-construction, Duveen showed Eva a fine selection of English furniture formerly owned by a nobleman. At Eva's insistence, Magaziner enlarged Wingwood's main room to hold the collection, which threw the entire project off balance; rescaling it enlarged the mansion even further.

It was in these lavishly appointed spaces, such as this garden room, that Eva Stotesbury entertained on a grand scale, with dinners for two hundred served on Limoges porcelain with sterling and gold silverware. It was not uncommon for her to orchestrate several events each week, keeping her core staff of forty moving at a nonstop pace.

Photo courtesy of the Mildred McCormick Estate

By 1929, Edward Stotesbury had achieved his goal, declaring his worth to be $100 million. One could see the results: three lavish estates, each containing its own art collection; several yachts; and many glittering jewels bestowed on Eva. The Stotesburys, along with fellow Philadelphian and millionaire radio inventor Atwater Kent, clutched onto the Gilded Age, extending its influence on Bar Harbor for just a few more years. They imprinted a social legacy, dubbed the "white-tie era" by some for its formal, elegant events. Though the Great Depression initially slowed the Stotesburys' spending, they soon resumed their $10 million annual sprees until Edward's death in 1938, which left Eva with insufficient funds to support even one of their houses. A mere $5 million remained. Fortunately for Eva, she died eight years before her beloved estate was leveled for the building of the present-day ferry terminal.

Photo courtesy of the Mildred McCormick Estate

Refined Amusements

THIS SIMPLE STRUCTURE with its natural pine columns doesn't reveal the original purpose of the Oasis Club—to create a place where rusticating gentlemen could converse while imbibing alcohol, Maine's then-forbidden drink. While visiting the state with the second-oldest Prohibition law, sojourners established Bar Harbor's first club in 1874 on the corner of School and Mount Desert streets.

Seven years later, the membership had outgrown this humble building, both in number and in sophistication. They purchased Alfred Veazie's cottage and renamed their organization the Mount Desert Reading Room. The organization flourished in this new location by the shore, growing to include 307 members. Outgrowing their quarters once again, they moved the former Veazie cottage to the corner of West and Bridge streets and hired Boston architect William R. Emerson to design a new clubhouse to match their national prestige.

Photograph courtesy of the Bar Harbor Historical Society

Mt. Desert Reading Rooms, Bar Harbor, Me.

EMERSON'S DESIGN fit the Mount Desert Reading Room's functions perfectly. From the club's broad piazza or any of the picturesque bay windows, the men and their guests could enjoy a view of Frenchman Bay and the Porcupine Islands while watching for arriving yachts. Inside the building they could discuss world events, read in any of the parlors or the library, or play pool in the billiard room. Knowing Maine's famous chilly weather, Emerson included fireplaces in all of the public rooms. By the new century, membership began to lag as the men started to enjoy socializing in their own cottages. By 1921, the three sole members began leasing out the building for other uses: a yacht club; a U.S. Naval headquarters during World War II; and, finally, an inn, which it remains today.

Photo courtesy of the Maine Historic Preservation Commission

IN 1878, when this photo of the Bar Harbor Cooking Club was taken, America was debating women's roles in society and the home. Some women wanted the freedom to become part of the male-dominated professions—teachers, doctors, journalists, and entrepreneurs—while others were happy to remain homemakers. Spurred on by *Mrs. Beeton's Book of Household Management* (1861), many women were interested in cooking, as was demonstrated by the number of summer club members shown in this photo: the Misses Murdock, Washington, Watson, Smith, Gardner, Balch, Beating, Drayton, Saunders, Nelson, and Pryne.

Twenty years later, ladies of the summer elite established their own social club, the Womens' Club nestled between the Newport House Hotel and the men's Reading Room. If the men were going to have their own exclusive club, so would the women!

Photo courtesy of the Bar Harbor Historical Society

NOW THIS "Who's Who of America's social elite" sought a centralized place to socialize and display their wealth. In other resorts, such as Saratoga Springs and Newport, cottagers had already built casinos and racetracks. Knowing that amenities such as these were needed in order for Bar Harbor to continue to attract America's aristocrats, cottagers Charles T. How, DeGrasse Fox, Ogden Codman, and others organized the Kebo Valley Club in 1888. Here, the community is gathering for a harness race at the one-mile track in front of the original clubhouse. This club set the tone for exclusive socializing for decades to come. The days of egalitarian entertainment that revolved around hotels had passed.

Photo courtesy of Raymond Strout

DeGrasse Fox probably influenced the decision to hire fellow Philadelphian Wilson Eyre to design the club building and gatehouse (shown above) of the Kebo Valley Club. These buildings were Eyre's first commissions in Maine, just six years after he began his architecture practice. According to one biography, "the Kebo represented a special plum for the architect as it gave him the opportunity to design a suitable enclosure for the social center of a self-consciously fashionable community."[1]

Eyre created a broad piazza, stretching the entire length of the 230-foot Shingle-style building, from which to view the horse races, golf and tennis games, and croquet matches below. Inside, members could enjoy plays in the theater, dances in the ballrooms, dinners and teas in the restaurant, or a quiet chat with a friend in front of a cozy fireplace. For the cart driver shown, a feast of activities awaited, as long as he was a member or guest.

Photo courtesy of the Maine Historic Preservation Commission

A LITTLE MORE than a decade after its opening, the original Kebo Valley Club burned, but the members lost no time in hiring local architect Fred Savage to construct the new clubhouse on the opposite bank of Bunker Hill. The fire had not reached the gatehouse, so Savage incorporated that structure into the new, rambling, Shingle-style clubhouse.

Savage designed the building to accommodate both large and small functions. Luncheons, teas, and dinners, hosted by members, filled the summer calendar, along with tournaments. Here, Edwardian ladies gathered in their flowing white cotton dresses and picturesque hats for the club's table tennis tournament on August 12, 1902. Later in the evening, once they had changed into their evening gowns, they could return to the club for a feast of clams, fillet of beef with a cherry sauce, pâté de foie gras, and roast grouse, finished with ice cream and cake—all for only $1.50.

Photo courtesy of the Bar Harbor Historical Society

THE HAIGHT FAMILY readies to see the island sights in a springy buckboard. A ride fifteen years earlier would have been a jarring experience in a high mountain wagon. W. H. Davis of Ellsworth is credited with designing the buckboard in the 1870s. The entry was low to the ground, and the carriage offered a pleasant, swaying ride through the scenery. While the passengers enjoyed the ride, the horses did all the work.

Bishop William Lawrence, a cottager, com-mented about the horse's duty, as the buckboard's "length made it heavy to haul, and three on each seat of four seats was a killing load, even for four horses."[2] Enterprising buckboard drivers charged passengers $1.50 for round-trip rides to Schooner Head, Otter Cliffs, and Eagle Lake. For the ride to the Green (Cadillac) Mountain summit, passengers often took pity on the horses and hiked up the last section to the top.

Photo courtesy of the Bar Harbor Historical Society

FROM THE 1870S ONWARD, buckboard rides and hikes often headed to the Jordan Pond House (shown at left), the modest teahouse on the southern shore of Jordan Pond. Patronage grew as the news spread of its delectable broiled chicken dinners and sumptuous pop-overs, offered in a picturesque setting. In 1895, Nellie and Thomas McIntire took over from the original proprietor, Melvin Tibbetts. Over the next two decades, the place expanded, adding dining rooms paneled with birch bark and cedar, a rock-faced fireplace for warmth on a chilly day, and a music room where concerts rivaled those held in neighboring Bar Harbor. By 1917, a columnist reported that "clear-eyed girls, maybe Northeastern marms, immaculate in snowy aprons, cuffs and collars served over 600 dinners in a day. The popovers were so good, and burning hot that a coin was quietly sent to the kitchen to secure a second portion . . . Never had I eaten more heartily."[3]

Photo courtesy of Raymond Strout

HORSE RIDING and driving played an important role in Bar Harbor society. Wanting to match Newport's horse show, prominent cottagers Major Edward Morrell, A. J. Cassatt, Philip Livingston, and others established a formal horse show in Robin Hood Park (the present Jackson Laboratory parking lot). For twelve years, this event closed out the official season.

Marion Lawrence describes her day at the 1901 show, where she had reserved seats in the grandstand: "A gay crowd of people on coaches, carriages and afoot, a band playing and the beautiful horses prancing up and down the track made a scene of color, life and gayety." She might have seen this Roof Seat Break carriage, led by a trio of fine Hackney horses. The lone groom has maneuvered the horses to a fine turnout before the judges' stand (at right).

Though horses would continue to dominate the transportation realm until 1913, the Bar Harbor horse show ceased after 1912.

Photo courtesy of Raymond Strout

AROUND 1910, the rivalry between various cottagers for the best-stocked stable escalated. Here, a governess and her young charge in their simple basket-style governess cart pose with their coachman, standing at attention, to show off their striking pony outside the Blair estate gates. Down the road, New York financier Ernesto Fabbri had stocked his stables with a handsome collection of eleven horses, many brought over from Europe, and a comparable number of carriages.

Some cottagers, such as Edward B. McLean, publisher of the *Washington Post*, set out to create a typical English estate, adding sheep, dogs, and chickens to his collection of prize-winning horses. No fine estate is complete without glittering jewels, so McLean purchased the Hope Diamond for his wife, which his family later donated to the Smithsonian.

Photo courtesy of the Maine Historic Preservation Commission

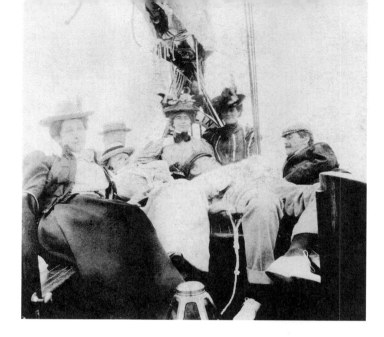

OVER TIME, YACHTING replaced canoeing as a favorite pastime in Bar Harbor. The seaport town, which had served as a base for the islanders' seafaring occupations for a century, was now speckled with pleasure boats of all sizes and styles. Some were owned by summer visitors, while others were rented for the season, complete with islander captains who remembered the days of fishing and boatbuilding along the shore.

As is evident in this photo showing Natalie Barney (in the dark hat), relaxing on a cruise with her friends in 1897, Bar Harbor continued to enjoy a less-formal social atmosphere and a greater *joie de vivre* than rival resorts.

Photo courtesy of Smithsonian Institution Archives

"WE DO NOT MINGLE enough with minds that influence the world," said the famous nineteenth-century Shakespearean actor Edwin Booth upon forming The Players Club for artists and their literary brethren in New York City. Brother to John Wilkes Booth, Edwin Booth (front row, center) surrounded himself with some of the brightest authors of the time: Thomas B. Aldrich (back left), Laurence Hutton (far right), and Parke Godwin (bearded, in front). New York banker "Commodore" E. C. Benedict (front left) hosted this cruise on his 138-foot steam yacht, *Oneida*. Actor Lawrence Barrett (black hat) and Rev. William Bispham, close friends of Booth's, shared his enthusiasm for the project. Bar Harbor cottager Parke Godwin, editor of the New York *Evening Post*, joined the group when they stopped at this resort. It was during this coastal tour in July 1887 that Booth decided to organize the club, which exists to this day on New York's Gramercy Square as a place for camaraderie among artists.

Photo courtesy of the Maine Historic Preservation Commission

EVEN LARGER than the *Oneida*, J. P. Morgan's 302-foot *Corsair III* (at right) was built at a cost of $3 million in 1898. The great financier did not own a cottage in Bar Harbor. Instead, he would visit the island on his floating palace. With a crew of around eighty to feed, each food-supply delivery from local grocers could total more than $1,000.

There was plenty of space for entertaining on board, and Morgan often would invite friends to join him for a cruise around the island. Marian Peabody remembers a luncheon on one of these cruises when the seas became choppy: "Mr. Morgan's very bright black eyes (with a somewhat mischievous gleam in them as they glanced around the table) would take note of the growing depression and finally he would say, 'Don't wait for me if anyone prefers the deck,' and here would be an immediate but dignified exit toward the companionway and fresh air."[4]

Photo courtesy of the Maine Historic Preservation Commission

DONNING PROFESSIONAL COOKING ATTIRE, these members of the exclusive Pot and Kettle Club gathered weekly to prepare a meal together and share tales and raucous jokes. Begun in 1898, the membership was kept to a manageable number of fifty, and some claim that in the early years, the group represented 85 percent of the wealth in the nation. The guest book reads like a "Who's Who" of politics and society, including presidents Taft and Theodore and Franklin D. Roosevelt; musicians Kreisler, Bauer, and Schelling; and author Arthur Train, famous for his amusing toasts. A few times each season, events would be open to women as well. Longtime cottager Marian Peabody remembers parties hosted by the genial Colonel Bush of Kentucky. "The Pot and Kettle was a perfect spot for his parties—in fact, for all entertaining, as the food was the best on the Island."[4]

Photo courtesy of Raymond Strout

LAURA BARNEY, bedecked, beaded, and bedazzled with sequins and tiger lilies, strikes a glamorous pose as Cleopatra, circa 1898. Wealthy aristocrats hosted extravagant dress balls and costume parties in this era, and no family was quite as famous for whimsical entertainments as the Barneys.

Cottagers took these entertainments seriously, as reported in the August 24, 1901, issue of the *New York Times*. For Mrs. Burton Harrison's Marie Antoinette–period costume party, cottager Ruth Lawrence ordered a silk gown from Paris, copied from a period painting showing Queen Marie Antoinette's court. If a socialite's daily life seemed like a fantasy to the common person, their parties took on a nearly unimaginable air of exotic privilege.[5]

Photo courtesy of Smithsonian Institution Archives

THE MEN in this elite group selected Bar Harbor native Fred Savage to design the Pot and Kettle clubhouse in 1900 on the shore overlooking Hulls Cove. Savage chose Shingle style, an indigenous architectural form, for the plans, creating open spaces lit with natural light, perfect for entertaining. The interior dining room, colorfully decorated with red and gold, was personalized with private yacht ensigns hung from the rafters. With the advent of the automobile, membership broadened over the years to include cottagers from all over the island.

Photo courtesy of the Maine Historic Preservation Commission

ON A CLOUDLESS AFTERNOON around 1905, members of the Swimming Club competed in a variety of water sports. The pool enclosure, filled with salt water from the bay, would warm with the sun's rays to a moderate temperature—warmer than the frigid ocean water, but chilly nonetheless.

This club, located on West Street, became the center for resort activities, especially for families with children, often accompanied by their governesses. At the annual water sports day, competitors from the Northeast Harbor Swim Club would visit to compete in a variety of creative races: canoe tug-of-war, tilting in canoes, men's and ladies' diving, a fancy race for mixed teams, and the 200-yard race for the Mount Desert Island championship.

In this photo, ladies in starched white dresses line the pool and the clubhouse terrace to watch the boys' diving competition. Members could have lunch on the lawn, serenaded by members of the Boston Symphony Orchestra hired for this purpose.

Photo courtesy of Raymond Strout

KINDERGARTEN TEACHER Alice Eastman oversees her cherubic summer students in 1897 (from left): Beatrice Chanler, Alice Whiting, Alice Damrosch, Bill and Margaret Schieffelin, Hester Chanler, Maurice Fremont-Smith, and Julia Whiting. Prominent summer families established this private kindergarten to help their children socialize with others and learn proper manners. In its early years, the class was held in private cottages such as Clearfield on Albert Meadow Lane, shown here. The girls and boys, all prim and proper in their white frocks and trim sailor suits, appear ready to learn good manners.

By 1912, the private kindergarten had expanded to fifty-nine children, including those from year-round families, and moved into its first permanent location. School director Evelyn Higgenbotham reported that the teachers taught the children about nature and nurturing, courtesy, and obedience in preparation for the larger duties and responsibilities in their future.[6]

Photo courtesy of the Bar Harbor Historical Society

THE EARLY RELIGIOUS SERVICES in Eden were held either in the meetinghouse in Hulls Cove, built in 1797, or in private houses, schools, and barns. With few horses, parishioners would walk to the service to hear a sermon preached by a visiting minister.

In Bar Harbor, residents built a white clapboard meetinghouse in 1860, where the Congregational Church now stands on Mount Desert Street. All the local denominations used this building until they had enough members to build separate places of worship, which would occur by 1883. In that year, the Congregationalists, having outgrown the hall, hired noted architect William R. Emerson to replace the simple New England–style building. Emerson borrowed characteristics from the Shingle style, such as dormered windows and simple lines, and combined them with arched windows and entranceways to produce the Romanesque-style church in this picture.

When this church burned in 1942, the Congregationalists returned to a traditional New England–style white church, which remains today.

Photo courtesy of the Maine Historic Preservation Commission

MANY OF THE PROMINENT early visitors to the island were Episcopalian, including Bishop Doane of Albany, a Northeast Harbor cottager, Bar Harbor's William Lawrence (later Bishop of Massachusetts), and Gouverneur M. Ogden. Maine's Bishop Neely visited in the 1870s, and his sermons attracted such a large gathering that services were moved to the Rodick House. The Episcopalians needed a church to call their own.

In 1878, the church council selected New York architect Charles C. Haight for the project. Previously he had designed St. Luke's Cathedral in Portland for Bishop Neely, followed by Ogden's summer residence. The new church was called St. Saviour's to honor the original French Jesuit mission that had settled on the island in the 1600s.

By 1886, a flourishing summer population necessitated a major expansion. This architectural rendering shows how Boston architects Rotch and Tilden added a nave to Haight's original church, transforming the original building into a transept.

Photo courtesy of the Maine Historic Preservation Commission

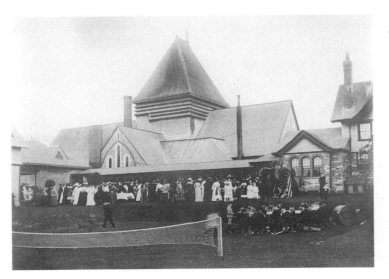

J. P. MORGAN personally assisted with plans for the Archbishop of Canterbury's 1904 visit to the United States, and to St. Saviour's Church in particular. Never before had an English archbishop visited America. Though the parishioners were accustomed to visiting preachers such as Boston's Philip Brooks, Harvard's President Eliot, or even their own Bishop Lawrence, this visit was an honor for the small community. The Bar Harbor band played during the reception, held in the church's back yard.

The Reverend Christopher Starr Leffingwell preached year-round to the parishioners of Bar Harbor. Marian Peabody, daughter of Bishop Lawrence, remembers the reverend well, describing him as "a saint, and looked it, with his deep-set eyes, erect carriage and long white beard. I always thought the prophets might have looked like him."[4]

Photo courtesy of Raymond Strout

Through this interior photograph of St. Saviour's, we can see both the Haight and the Rotch and Tilden plans. Rotch and Tilden reoriented the original Haight church and added on the nave and the apse area through the arches at the rear. With this transformation, the building's architectural character changed from High Victorian Gothic to Romanesque Revival, with Shingle-style elements. These changes resulted in a more elaborate church. The Florentine marble altar, donated by Mrs. Ogden, would be added later, as would the ten Tiffany windows memorializing several parishioners.

Photo courtesy of the Maine Historic Preservation Commission

This Catholic church, St. Silvia, stood on the bank of Kebo Street in large part due to the efforts of Philadelphians DeGrasse Fox and Brooke White, who donated the land and solicited plans from noted architect William R. Emerson. Ignoring the trend toward the Gothic style for churches, Emerson chose the Shingle style for his design in order to make its parishioners feel welcome and at home.

According to architectural historian Roger Reed, St. Silvia is notable for its tower, topped by an arched belfry, and its spire, inspired by the Old Ship Meeting House in Hingham, Massachusetts. The island community, including Native Americans, raised $2,600 to build the church. In 1882, the *Mount Desert Herald* noted that "The Indians in particular responded almost without exception, appearing to consider it a privilege to contribute from their scanty means to such an object."[7]

Photo courtesy of the Maine Historic Preservation Commission

As the summer colony grew, so too did the number of domestic servants, many of whom were Roman Catholic immigrants from Ireland. In the early 1900s, St. Silvia needed to be expanded to meet the worshiping needs of the community, and they chose Victor Hodgins of Bangor to design a Gothic Revival–style church, later renamed Holy Redeemer. By selecting Hodgins to prepare the design, the congregation was making a status statement. This impressive building, with its imposing square granite tower, stood directly across Mount Desert Street from the stone St. Saviour's Episcopal Church and a block from the Congregational Church. The style was typical of early-twentieth-century churches. Today, the church looks much the same and continues to provide worship services to parishioners.

Photo courtesy of the Maine Historic Preservation Commission

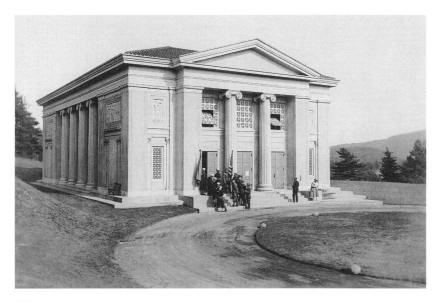

By the early 1900s, Bar Harbor sought to become a mecca for artists. Boston architect Guy Lowell, having recently designed Boston's Museum of Fine Arts, seemed an obvious choice to plan the new Building of the Arts. Lowell designed a neoclassical temple-style theater sheathed in stucco, but with an appearance of marble, set against a wooded backdrop and overlooking the Kebo Valley Club. Completed in 1907, the temple was an immediate success, attracting nationally known musicians, symphony orchestras, dancers, and theater companies each summer. An amphitheater built into the natural hillside behind the arts building provided a perfect setting for Shakespeare plays and other enlightening outdoor entertainments for vacationing intellectuals.

Photo courtesy of the Maine Historic Preservation Commission

By World War I, the arts temple was attracting world-class musicians, as evidenced by this 1919 photograph. Some in this jovial group have switched instruments to fool the unknowing. Pianist Harold Bauer is holding the instrument of flutist George Barrère (seated at his left), while a female musician plays Carlos Salzedo's harp as he stands to her left. Cellist Paul Kéfer has lent his cello to the musician immediately to his right, while tenor George Harris Jr. (seated at right) and pianist Josef Hofmann (far right) are empty-handed.

Performances provided a way to raise money for war charities. By the late 1930s, even though stars from Hollywood and Broadway appeared on the temple stage, fewer seats were filled. In harder times, the building was also used for local events, such as the 1930 Graduation Class Day for Bar Harbor High School; graduate Elizabeth Gorer described the place as "dreamy." Maintenance requirements outgrew the budget eventually, and the building closed in 1939. In a final dramatic performance, the temple burned in the flames of the 1947 fire.

Photo courtesy of the Bar Harbor Historical Society

When the yellow silk curtains were drawn on opening night at the Building of the Arts, opera prima donna Emma Eames and her husband, Emilio de Gorgoza, of the Metropolitan Opera serenaded the four hundred guests seated in these chairs, and in the private box seats above. During intermission, the audience could appreciate the neoclassical architectural features that surrounded them, the subdued red and light blue color scheme, the recessed panels dotting the ceiling that beamed lights downward, and the towering glass windows that provided natural light and a splendid view of the surrounding hills.

For its first two decades, the temple provided world-class entertainment to Bar Harbor's summer colony. At times, local residents who could afford the tickets would also attend the concerts. "If we wanted to see a performance, we would have to go in through the back," remarked local resident Marianne Stanley. Fred Salisbury, groundskeeper at Kebo, recalled that on rainy days, he and fellow workers assigned to clean up the theater "would be up there singing. It had great acoustics."

Photo courtesy of the Maine Historic Preservation Commission

"WHEN YOU RODE the Bar Harbor Express, you had the distinct feeling that you belonged to a very select coterie, to be found only in an equally select location. And you were right on both accounts," writes Roger B. Buettell in his 1967 *Yankee* magazine article. Before 1884, travelers used only steamers and carriages to get to Bar Harbor. This changed in June 1884, when the Maine Central Railroad established a new terminus at Mount Desert Ferry, across Frenchman Bay from Bar Harbor. Riders would take the train to this new terminal, and a steamer then ferried them across to Bar Harbor.

Bar Harbor's elite expected luxury and efficiency, which was provided by the all-Pullman-car Express. Both Alexander Cassatt and George W. Pullman, cottagers at Bar Harbor, would arrive in their own Pullman cars. For those who could not afford the train, steamers still provided an affordable option.

Photo courtesy of Earl Brechlin

IT WAS NOT UNCOMMON for the Kebo Valley Club to host celebrities, as it did on July 22, 1910, when the portly President Taft played golf with Captain Archibald Butts and the shorter John L. Ketterlinus, president of the club. "Apparently, [Taft] is determined to get all the enjoyment possible from the Kebo links and he finds them well worth the long trip here," reported a *New York Times* columnist.

In the first two decades of the 1900s, the Kebo maintained its status as the center of social life, though horse racing events had moved to Robin Hood Park. By this time women were also being allowed to take swings on the links at Kebo. Local boys such as Howard Clark (at left), earned money caddying for these wealthy socialites. Resident Nan Cole reported that the seventeenth hole frustrated the President, earning the nickname "Howard Taft's Nemesis."

Photo courtesy of the Bar Harbor Historical Society

WHEN TAFT ARRIVED at the Village Green, he found a well-manicured lawn surrounding an Italian fountain and the bandstand from which he was to speak—if they could manage to get the rotund president up the ladder. The Green was just one of the Village Improvement Association's (VIA) projects designed to beautify the area. What had been the site of the Grand Central Hotel was now a green designed for public enjoyment. Summer residents had organized the VIA in 1881 to improve Bar Harbor's sanitation, roads, public works, and overall aesthetics.

In the 1920s, tensions arose between the islanders and the summer colony over the musical entertainment offered by the Bar Harbor band and members of the Boston Symphony Orchestra. They reached a compromise that split the time between the locals and the professionals—four nights for the Bar Harbor musicians, and three nights for the Symphony. As historian Lynne Nelson Manion notes, "It was a defining moment for the town when local musicians stepped aside in deference to talented visiting professionals."[8]

Photo courtesy of the Maine Historic Preservation Commission

IN THIS 1921 PHOTO, local band members posed to commemorate their group, and some can be identified today. From left to right, first row: Fred Higgins, Fred Wescott, Warren Curtin, Gleason Farrar (boy), John Hinch, [unidentified], William Graham, [two unidentified]. From left to right, second row: [unidentified], Fuller Foster, Ralph Higgins, Donald Dyer, [unidentified], Charles Holt. From left to right, third row: "Puss" Ingalls, Horace Dow, [unidentified], Ralph Talbot, [unidentified], Gilley Foster, [unidentified]. Last row: unidentified except for Horace Pettengill at far right.

Though reports of the band date back to as early as 1875, when it had sixteen members, the group had a shaky start, reorganizing several times between then and 1887, when Dr. J. T. Hinch (standing front center, with cornet) became the bandleader. New life was breathed into the band's existence with the construction of a hall on Main Street. Though their headquarters would shift to several different locations on Main Street, one could always find the band performing at the Village Green on summer evenings. Elizabeth Akers Allen remembered those evenings fondly: "I loved the band concerts. I ran and danced around the bandstand until I fell exhausted to the ground."

Photo courtesy of the Bar Harbor Historical Society

WHEN HERBERT W. GLEASON, the Park Service's first photographer, took this picture during a performance of *Young Leonardo* at Dorr's Old Farm in August 1917, he captured a typical summer entertainment for Bar Harbor society. Guests had paid $2 per ticket to see the actors depict Leonardo da Vinci's boyhood, to enjoy tea under the Italianate pergola, and to have their fortunes read. Proceeds benefited Edith Wharton's war charities to aid French refugees and soldiers. *Tableaux vivants* were another popular summer entertainment, in which participants would re-create the subjects of famous paintings on the stage.

Photo courtesy of the William Otis Sawtelle Collections, Acadia National Park

HOLLYWOOD'S VIKINGS and mermaids visited Bar Harbor in 1917 for the filming of the Fox Company's *Queen of the Sea*, producer John G. Adolfi. The cast of a hundred or so moved into the St. Sauveur Hotel, although the queen, played by newly minted star Annette Kellerman, and her assembly of servants preferred a cottage. Although Bar Harbor socialites were initially reserved when it came to mingling with the cast members, their tune soon changed, as reported by the *Bar Harbor Times*: "'Why, the motion picture people look and act like perfectly normal people,' society agreed after a careful survey with lorgnette and field glass." To which the actors replied, "Millionaires are human." Soon, society was courting the cast with parties, dances, and picnics, and many rusticators clustered on the rocks to watch the filming. At one point more than two hundred cars hovered around the location, and spectators enjoyed the view while feasting on picnics—so-called "rock parties."

Photo courtesy of the Bar Harbor Historical Society

PRINCESS LEANDRA, played by Mildred Keats, tries to coax the mermaid queen, played by Annette Kellerman, into the water, while six-year-old Virginia Higgins of Bar Harbor looks on. Others besides Virginia joined in the production of *Queen of the Sea* as extras, but the impact of the filming did not stop there. It was estimated that over the two months, the area benefited by more than $75,000, not including the donations to the local hospital made by selling tickets to view the filming as it occurred. During their stay, the Southern California mermaids and mermen adapted to the rugged Maine out-croppings, the cold water, and the friendly harbor seals, and when the filming ended, it was a sad departure. Mount Desert Island's dramatic scenery drew Hollywood back a few more times in the following years.

Photo courtesy of the Bar Harbor Historical Society

For society children such as brothers Valentine and J. Noel Macy, romping on the lawn still entailed wearing their summer whites. In this era (c. 1901), donning crisp white shorts or dresses signaled elite status, and many small boys were attired in dresses during their early years. Children doing head-stands on the soft green grass meant a laun-dress spending hours over a kettle of boiling water, scrubbing out the grass stains and then pressing the garment to perfection.

Regimented routines guided the summer children through their days: swim lessons at the club, home for lunch, afternoon hikes or visits, and possibly an outing in the evening; if not, they would stay at home with the nanny.

Photo courtesy of the Bar Harbor Historical Society

J. Noel Macy, grandson of Josephine Carpenter and son of millionaire industrialist V. Everit Macy, ponders Janus, the Roman god of beginnings and endings. It is the first decade of the twentieth century, and Bar Harbor has witnessed the transformation of the village from a quiet working town to a bustling watering hole for the rich, rivaling Newport as the nation's premier summer resort. The question to ponder: Was the summer colony beginning a new era, or nearing the end of one?

Photo courtesy of the Bar Harbor Historical Society

Relaxing at a ledgy island summit, industrialist V. Everit Macy, son-in-law of Mrs. Miles Carpenter, enjoys the panoramic view of land and sea at his feet. Just like his son in the previous photo, V. Everit Macy enjoyed the island, yet father and son would experience it in different ways. Macy Sr. enjoyed the luxuries of Bar Harbor life, including a house full of servants, several exclusive clubs, horseback riding, dinners, and dances. He also took advantage of the island's beauty by hiking up the mountains; he enjoyed the feel of solid rock under his feet. His son would enjoy these natural pleasures too, but extravagant lifestyles waned during his time. By the 1920s, the nation had been to war and was now paying for it through the income tax. Bit by bit, the financial squeeze would change the lives of most families, drawing the Gilded Age to a close.

Photo courtesy of the Bar Harbor Historical Society

New Occupations

THIS EARLY PHOTOGRAPH SHOWS the shore of Bar Harbor around 1878. At the left of the wharf are the cottages and stables of the Hardy and Veazie families. The Rockaway Hotel looms above the sailboats. Visitors could have a bath in the long low building on the shore. Along Main Street, then a narrow dirt road, stands the Agamont House on the right and the Newport Hotel on the left. With turrets pointing to the sky, the Grand Central Hotel vies with the mansard-topped towers of the Rodick House for the right to be named the tallest building in town, while at right, one can see the homes of the local villagers, shipbuilders, lumbermen, and fishermen. Ten years hence, this skyline would look radically different as the nation's elite built summer houses and the locals built more hotels.

Photo courtesy of the Maine Historic Preservation Commission

As this c. 1885 map shows, the area now known as Bar Harbor was growing rapidly, with shops, houses, cottages, manufacturers, churches, mills, and other services clustered along the downtown streets. West Street consisted of only two blocks, with the posh West End Hotel dominating the landscape. Andover Seminary professor Austin Phelps's cottage stood at the end, with worker housing built between it and the shore.

A combination of permanent resident housing, cottages, and businesses dotted both Cottage and Mount Desert streets. In the summer, locals would move in with relatives, renting their own homes to summer people and pocketing a good profit in just a few months.

During this period, Eden's population soared by almost 300 percent, to 4,379 people. The valuation of property exploded to almost $7 million, an increase of more than 1,000 percent. Prosperity for almost all had arrived.

Photo courtesy of the Maine Historic Preservation Commission

STANDING OUTSIDE the American Express Company on West Main Street (c. 1880), this carriage is ready to deliver its cargo of trunks, hatboxes, suitcases, and other freight to homes and businesses in Bar Harbor. In the late nineteenth century, the U.S. Postal Service only accepted letters and did not guarantee delivery. People depended on freight services to ship their goods and possessions.

The only other communications method at this time, besides letter writing, was the telegraph. The Bar Harbor and Mount Desert Telegraph opened in 1871 with two operators. Most people, including Joseph Pulitzer, used telegraphs for "quick" communication. Mr. Pulitzer's daily routine of sending and receiving telegraphs from his office kept delivery boys busy. "One of the best summer jobs in town was that of a Western Union messenger; he would deliver a telegram, receive 50 cents, then wait outside a few minutes, before hurrying to the door with another message for another 50 cents."[1]

Photo courtesy of the Maine Historic Preservation Commission

THE CHILDREN OF William and Maria Schieffelin are dwarfed by the family's steamer trunks as they stand ready to head back to New York after summering on the island. These descendants of the Vanderbilt and Schieffelin families were not atypical in their travel packing. When the aristocratic families arrived for the summer, they brought sturdy steamer trunks packed full of dresses, hats, parasols, gloves, books, special picture frames, and letter-writing packets—all of life's comforts for their stay.

By the 1890s, fashionable women were expected to have several changes of clothes for each day: loose-fitting tea gowns for morning and late-afternoon receiving times, and day dresses for Kebo Valley Club luncheons and whist parties. The more cumbersome and restrictive day outfits were not complete without an elegant hat and parasol. For the evening dances and performances, women brought with them a variety of bustled gowns and glittering jewels. Once the trunks were unpacked, the festivities could begin.

Photo courtesy of the Bar Harbor Historical Society

FOR VISITORS stepping off of the SS *Mount Desert* around 1885, this part of West Main Street, just beyond Tobias Roberts's Agamont House, was their introduction to Bar Harbor village. A stroll along the noisy plank sidewalk brought the traveler to Berry's Store, which offered a range of goods, from rocking chairs to oats. Next door, tin makers Green & Reynolds provided an assortment of stoves, pots, and pans. If footwear was needed for climbing the mountains, S. C. Vyles could fit the customer to a pair of sturdy shoes. Farther up the street, the gents could stop in at Charles Pineo's hall for a round of billiards, while the ladies strolled on to the Rodick House for lunch or tea.

The scene pictured here is uncommonly quiet. On a busy summer day, Marion Crawford described a host of tintype artists and booths with sandwiches and temperance beverages set up along this short stretch.[2]

Photo courtesy of the Maine Historic Preservation Commission

AFTER TEA at the Rodick House, a visitor could cross the street and venture along this stretch of Main Street, from the Bradley Block at the farthest point to Sproul's Café at right. In 1879, photographer Bryant Bradley built the three-story building at the end of this block, opened his studio, and leased the remaining space. With a stop at T. L. Roberts's store or R. A. Sproul's Market, anything from grain to cigars to canned goods could be purchased, and if one was looking for a newspaper or fine confectionary, Bee's Store, standing mid-row, was well stocked.

Bar Harbor's first restaurant, Sproul's Café (at right), became so popular with the society's upper crust that it earned the title "Delmonico's of the North." After a walk up from the wharf and along both sides of Main Street, the Grand Central Hotel across the street would be a welcome sight for the weary traveler.

Photo courtesy of the Maine Historic Preservation Commission

SHOPKEEPER ALBERT W. BEE and his family led a nomadic life during the 1880s and '90s. Mr. Bee, an entrepreneur from California, began his working life in Bar Harbor selling newspapers on the steamer wharf. As profits accumulated, he opened a stationery store on Main Street, selling writing paper, candy, and newspapers during the summer months. With letter writing the major form of communication, his business expanded to all of the island's summer resorts.

As fall arrived and the rusticators left the island, so did Bee and his family. They moved to Boston to run their suburban Boston store, and for the holiday season he operated another store in the fashionable Temple Place district of Boston. As the weather warmed, the *Mount Desert Herald* would report, "Spring soon to come. Mr. Bee visited, but neither one bee nor one butterfly makes a summer."[3] Though Bee's store still exists today, Mr. Bee left permanently for sunnier West Coast shores in 1914.

Photo courtesy of Alice Corcoran

THE SERIOUS-LOOKING STAFF of John F. Hodgkins's fish market has prepared a stack of perfectly filleted fish, wrapped and ready for delivery. Owner John Hodgkins (at far left) kept the books, while Hallee Hodgkins, Morris Guptill, and George Salsbury (at right) wrapped the fish and served the customers. Wielding long knives at the far right are Frank Masher, Jim Carrigan, and Harrison Hodgkins.

At one time Bar Harbor fishermen exported their dried and salted fish to East Coast ports, but as Bar Harbor developed into a summer resort they found a market for their catch right at home. By the late 1890s, Hodgkins's business was just one of four fishmongers selling to cottagers. These markets not only sold locally harvested fish, but also imported fancy varieties for the sophisticated palates of their wealthy customers.

Photo courtesy of the Bar Harbor Historical Society

[previous page] THIS PHOTOGRAPH OFFERS a panoramic view of the variety of buildings nestled together in the town during the late 1800s. Prior generations had cut down the trees for lumber, so the view is unobstructed.

At one time, this area had belonged to the Higgins family, descendants of pioneer islander Israel Higgins. His children had made bricks, built ships, dried fish, chopped down trees, and farmed on these lands. Now one found homes, stores, stables, service providers, and, most important, many hotels. Hostelry provided a good living. In 1886, the local newspaper recorded that the West End proprietor had netted $13,000 in one season—but this success for large hotels was not to last.

In this view, the turreted Grand Central Hotel towers above E. Brewer's white farmhouse on the left. In 1899, the Grand Central was torn down; several years later, the community turned the spot into an open gathering place, the Village Green.

Photo courtesy of the Maine Historic Preservation Commission

In the 1870s, horses were still a rarity on the island, and oxen provided the power to pull work carts, plow fields, and even to move houses. Thrifty Mainers were known for their tendency to move houses rather than tear them down. Without the advantage of modern technology, these industrious men would use oxen to pull buildings through the streets to their new location.

In this case, the ox has a much lighter load—some furniture destined for a new home, possibly the Ocean House at rear. That small hotel, owned by Samuel Higgins, was located around the corner from Bradley's photo studio, on what is now Field Cottage Road.

Photo courtesy of the Maine Historic Preservation Commission

"What perseverance, pluck, and energy will do is exemplified in the advance made in the mercantile life of Bar Harbor's most successful dry goods merchant, Max Franklin." So commented the *Bar Harbor Record* on May 21, 1891. Standing in the doorway of his new store, Franklin might have been reflecting on his modest beginnings as a German immigrant. After two years of selling goods door to door in Bar Harbor, he partnered with an Ellsworth merchant to open a small store. His growing business soon led him to open his new store on Main Street, almost opposite the Grand Central Hotel.

Franklin, his son, Morris E. (at left), and his brother Morris, a shoe-store salesman (at right), were the earliest Jews in Bar Harbor. Over the years, their numbers would expand, but they never built a synagogue on the island. Instead, they either celebrated their faith in their homes or traveled to Bangor.

Photo courtesy of the Maine Historic Preservation Commission

MAX FRANKLIN and his wife, Annie, opened their store at a time when ready-made garments and mass-produced goods were beginning to replace handmade items. Women became more conscious of dressing in vogue, spurring an increase in U.S. production of women's clothing by 673 percent between 1880 and 1905. Simultaneously, the manufacture of hats quadrupled. Sellers such as the Franklins prospered as they offered blouses, dresses, cloaks, hats, fabrics, linens, gloves, rugs, and a host of other goods.

The Franklins were not the only dry goods merchants in Bar Harbor, however; two local women and two men also opened stores that offered similar goods, providing plenty of shopping options for islanders and tourists alike.

Photo courtesy of the Bar Harbor Historical Society

BOSTONIAN John Haskell Butterfield opened his market as a franchise of Boston's Faneuil Hall Market in 1898. Running a store that catered to summer people was challenging. Its fifteen staff members worked from morning until night in the high season, filling cooks' orders from cottages and yachts. It was not uncommon for cottagers in the Gilded Age to host dinners for several hundred people, which meant placing a large order at Butterfield's. It was said that Butterfield's four meat cutters prepared more meat than any other grocer this side of Boston. Managers kept precise records of the orders because cottagers did not pay their bills until the end of the season. This meant that Mr. Butterfield paid for his stock and staff out of profits from the previous year.

Butterfield's mantra came true: If a business can survive for two years and make it through the third year, it will be here for life. Butterfield's continues on Main Street today.

Photo courtesy of John Wall

WITH THEIR MODEST RENDITION of a Tournament of Roses parade float, Butterfield's decorated their entry with grape vines covered with plump fruit, a perched raptor, and carnations in an overall patriotic tone. Marian L. Peabody recalls, "The '90s were the days of Flower Parades of ladies driving their own phaetons completely covered with flowers, from the horses' ears to the groom's seat in the back, including the lady herself, who wore a dress to match or contrast the flowers she had chosen for decoration."[4]

At the end of the season, John Butterfield and his family would leave Bar Harbor to open their Palm Beach store in time for the influx of winter visitors at that resort. The Butterfields and the Bees, mentioned earlier, were not the only families who migrated seasonally to operate businesses in two different locations. The Testas, another entrepreneurial Bar Harbor family, followed the same plan, with a caravan of seventeen people making the annual pilgrimage between Bar Harbor and Florida, where they operated a restaurant. Though this was a profitable routine, it meant that the children missed the beginning and end of each school year.

Photo courtesy of John Wall

WILLIAM H. SHERMAN personified the scholarly man. Born across the bay, in Sullivan, and educated in the public schools there, Sherman began his career as an office boy for the *Mount Desert Herald*, Bar Harbor's first newspaper. He soon opened a small stationery store and, a few years later, a printing company. Besides running the printing business, he was an Associated Press correspondent for twenty-two years. He also served as editor of the area's second and third newspapers, the *Bar Harbor Record* and the *Bar Harbor Times*, and would occasionally publish his own poems in the papers. A quiet and serious man, Sherman was dedicated to his new town, and served in the Maine Legislature. He was especially passionate about lifting the ban on automobiles in Bar Harbor—a battle he won!

Photo courtesy of Bar Harbor Masonic Lodge

FOR MORE THAN A CENTURY, Sherman's Books and Stationery has supplied customers with writing paper, books, ink, and, later, gifts. Sherman's first shop was located in the Hamor Block across from the Grand Central Hotel, but he soon moved to Cottage Street when his printing business expanded. By 1914, both businesses were flourishing. The Press Company published the *Bar Harbor Times* and smaller jobs, while the stationery store enjoyed a steady flow of customers, even in the winter. Though the town also had a public library, Sherman established a lending library in his store, charging two cents a day to borrow a book, with a minimum charge of 5 cents, a disadvantage for slow readers. After his death in 1928, two of his daughters ran the store for almost four decades, expanding its selection and moving it back to Main Street before selling it to Michael and Patricia Curtis. It remains in the Curtis family today.

Photo courtesy of Jeff Curtis

MADAME SANTIN stands by the door of the boutique she ran with seamstress Madame Blanpain (c. 1899), talking with Irving Mitchell while staff stand ready to welcome new clients.

In pre-industrial America, women predominantly worked at home. This situation changed with the opening of the weaving mills in the 1820s. By 1880, women were employed in 284 branches of industry.[5] Though men had dominated the millinery industry until the early 1800s, a century later it was women's turn. In an era of elaborate fashion displays, vogue dressers depended on seamstresses and milliners to outfit them appropriately. By 1901, nine dressmakers and six milliners offered their services to Bar Harbor's elite, though none created quite as sophisticated an image as Madame Santin and her seamstress counterpart, Madame Blanpain. These professions offered those with the necessary skills a way to achieve economic independence, as well as a respectable social status.

Photo courtesy of Raymond Strout

IN 1888, WHEN Helen M. Smith (shown here) was teaching in her own private Bar Harbor school, she introduced a new feature: current events reports. A few years later, she became a reporter for the *Bar Harbor Record*, initially as their Boston correspondent. Her tenure came to an abrupt end when Dr. Gilman Colby of Ellsworth purchased the paper and fired the young journalist. Undeterred, Smith moved to Boston and wrote for the *Boston Home Journal*, which "served as a pleasant and profitable school of journalism."[6] Colby's rule at the *Record* lasted only eighteen months. With $1,000 advanced to her by summer residents, Smith returned to Bar Harbor in 1893, purchased the paper, and became managing editor, an unusual position for a woman at that time. During her two decades as owner of the paper, she turned the tables and wrote about the students she had once taught.

Photo courtesy of the Maine Historic Preservation Commission

IN MAY 1898, members of the Bar Harbor Business Club, dressed in office attire, relaxed on Rodick (now Bar) Island for a clambake. The hectic season was approaching, so it was time to reflect on the good times they had enjoyed during the past winter. A variety of organizations provided fellowship for village men: the Masonic Lodge, the Independent Order of Odd Fellows (IOOF), the Knights of Pythias, the James M. Parker Post (Grand Army of the Republic), church groups, and special-interest clubs such as the one shown here. Some of these groups, such as the Masons and the IOOF, had their own halls, while others met in public buildings. Funds raised by their philanthropic activities—including carnivals, dances, and solicitations—filled Santa's bag with gifts during the holidays and enabled the hospital to extend its services to more people.

Photo courtesy of the Bar Harbor Historical Society

THIS GATHERING represents a small portion of the crew that built the Turrets between 1893 and 1895. In earlier days, some of these men had sailed on coasting and fishing vessels, but now they honed their residential building skills for better wages and more time at home. No longer were they spending months at a time away at sea. Instead, they were at the construction site for ten-hour days, six days a week, earning about two dollars per day.

With the advent of modern technologies, the building trades expanded accordingly. Electricians wired this cottage with more than 150 incandescent lights, so that at night it seemed like an Oriental palace when viewed from the water. The demands of sophisticated cottagers kept the plumbers up-to-date on the latest heating advances. When out-of-town craftsmen were brought in on cottage jobs, local trades benefited from learning their techniques. All of the trades were challenged with satisfying the demands of their wealthy clients.

Photo courtesy of College of the Atlantic

JOHN CLARK, originally from Surry, Maine, began his career in Bar Harbor as the contractor for the West End Hotel. The owner stipulated that the building needed to be completed in seventy-five days. Clark beat that mandate, with more than nine days to spare. Among the three hundred or so cottages he designed or built in the area, the Turrets and Stanwood are probably his best-known construction jobs. He was well known for his engineering skills. When the Marlborough Hotel needed to be moved three blocks down Main Street and out-of-town firms refused the job, Clark planned and supervised the move without a hitch.

One of Clark's competitors, Asa Hodgkins, was also known for expediting projects and for his genial nature. From his first job building the Des Isles Brothers store on Main Street, to St. Saviour's Church, the Pot and Kettle Club, Archbold Cottage, and almost all the cottages in neighboring Seal Harbor, Hodgkins's skill won him great acclaim.

Photo courtesy of the Maine Historic Preservation Commission

AT THEIR LOWER MAIN STREET business, twenty-one serious men, one pint-sized apprentice, and a lap-sized mascot joined their employers, Henry A. Lawford and H. E. Wakefield, to celebrate their recently formed business partnership with a formal photo portrait. Lawford and Wakefield's enterprise was just one of the seven painting and wallpapering businesses in Bar Harbor. The construction boom of the 1880s and '90s spurred the formation of many secondary trades, including plasterers, painters, and finish carpenters.

A local competitor, Frank Foster, offered several specialties to meet the tastes of his fashionable clientele. His frescoers could design a unique wall treatment sure to be admired by other socialites, and the owner himself specialized in enameling and gilding furniture, signs, and trim—an appropriate skill for the Gilded Age.

Photo courtesy of Raymond Strout

As the cottagers left for their winter homes, the cadence of life in Bar Harbor moderated. Renovating and maintaining buildings, putting the gardens to bed, and repairing roads kept workers busy.

Ice harvesters, who had to wait for the coldest winter temperatures to begin their work, would have used sleds like this to haul ice or equipment. In the 1880s, lumberman and blacksmith Daniel Brewer began harvesting ice from local ponds. Spike-shod horses pulled ice plows to cut deep grooves in the ice, after which his forty-five workers cut these strips into blocks, each weighing about 235 pounds. Insulated by sawdust, these gigantic cakes were stored in icehouses until the warmer months, when they were hauled to residents' iceboxes to preserve food. With the introduction of the electric refrigerator in the 1930s, the ice industry disappeared and the island's ponds once again became the province of ice fishermen and skaters in winter.

Photo courtesy of the Bar Harbor Historical Society

Watering was just one of Frank Anthony's responsibilities as gardener for the Satterlees' 110-acre estate at Great Head. The land had been a wedding gift to Mrs. Satterlee from her father, J. P. Morgan. The Great Head cottage was adorned with decorative landscaping; there was a huge vegetable garden to provide food for the family, servants, and guests; a cutting garden kept all the vases in the house supplied with flowers; and there were often several greenhouses on the grounds as well. Anthony tended all of this with the help of four assistants, living year-round with his family in a modest house on the property.

Each summer, ten servants accompanied the Satterlee family to the island: a personal maid, the butler, the cook, the kitchen maid, the parlor maid, two chauffeurs, two laundresses, and the pantry maid—a small number compared to the Stotesburys' thirty live-in servants.

Photo courtesy of the Bar Harbor Historical Society

Dressed for the occasion in her black taffeta uniform with white collar, cuffs, and lace-trimmed apron, one of Miss Mildred McCormick's maids stood ready to serve hors d'oeuvres to the guests. Prior to a party, the domestic staff would be in a flurry of activity—especially the superintendent, butler, and cook. These three staff people held greater seniority because they hired and fired the other workers. As Frederick Salisbury, groundskeeper at the Kebo Valley Club, described it, "Being the superintendent of one of those estates is like being a town manager . . . You've got everything to take care of . . . roads, the woods, all the gardens, [and] all the buildings are your responsibility."[7] Many people worked for the same families for years, and in some cases, all their lives. While for some this resulted in a familial relationship between employer and staff, the bond between them was always limited by an aura of reserve.

Photo courtesy of the Mildred McCormick Estate

The suited-up driver of this posh buckboard waits patiently for his customers outside the Jordan Pond House around the early 1900s. During this decade, more than thirteen liveries served Bar Harbor, and they ranged in size from a few hands to more than a hundred. Buckboards could be hired by the hour or for the day, and one could usually be found waiting beside the town clock on the Village Green. Heavy horses (like the ones shown here) were needed to pull buckboards loaded with rusticators along the hilly island roads.

Photo courtesy of Raymond Strout

AT THE STAFFORD BROTHERS livery stable, one could identify the owners, George and Andrew Jr., by their distinctive British accents. Along with their parents, they had immigrated to Bar Harbor from Berwick-on-Tweed, England, in 1886 and established this livery while still in their twenties. The partnership did not last, however. George Stafford continued on alone to establish the largest livery business in the state. His brother bought the Cleaves Brothers Stable on Main Street, while the original owners, L. Sherman Cleaves and Alonzo W. Cleaves, went on to specialize in veterinary surgery.

In 1893, Bar Harbor could boast 600 livery horses in the town, not including privately owned horses, of which there were many. When the rusticators' private horses arrived on the ferry, it created quite a spectacle, especially by 1899 when more than 1,000 horses clopped down steamer gangplanks, escorted by their grooms.

Photo courtesy of Raymond Strout

PATRIOTIC BUNTING draped George Stafford's livery building on the day this staff photograph was taken. Two of the coachmen were gallantly attired for the occasion, while the rest of Stafford's groomsmen, stablemen, and drivers were dressed according to their tasks.

Pamela Stafford, the owner's daughter, born in 1895, remembers her father's stables with "over 200 horses and about 100 men working for him. [He] had his own blacksmith shop and what they called a cookhouse where the men were fed. All on Cottage Street."[8] In the winter, the horses would be moved to a 600-acre farm with a big barn in Trenton, on the mainland.

Stafford's Bar Harbor stable burned to the ground in one hour in 1909. Though his horses were safe in Trenton at the time, all his carriages and harnesses were lost in the flames. Horses and carriages would continue to dominate the island roads for a few more years until the automobile took over in 1913.

Photo courtesy of Raymond Strout

AT THE KEBO VALLEY FIELD, two men stand ready to pitch the cut hay onto the growing mound. In rural areas, haying was a family event because it had to be dried and put under cover quickly to prevent it from rotting. One person would gather the cut hay into windrows with a horse-drawn dump rake like the one at left in this photo. Then men and women would pitch it into wagons, or, later, trucks. Children were especially fond of jumping in the mounds of sweet hay.

During the Civil War, or when male family members were off at sea, it was left to the women to run the homestead, including putting up the hay. After the war, as Bar Harbor's economic base switched to tourism, harvesting again became more difficult because it coincided with the height of the social season. The temporary help farmers had previously relied on were serving tourists instead. Despite the impediments, harvesting continued as an annual event into the 1940s, to the delight of energetic children.

Photo courtesy of the Bar Harbor Historical Society

ON A HOT, DRY DAY, one would probably have found these two gentlemen riding around the dusty Bar Harbor streets in T. L. Roberts's sprinkler tanker. The town appropriated $800 annually for the service. In 1888, villagers cried out for a second sprinkler to beat down the dust.

The ice delivery wagons left their own trickles of water on the dusty summer roads. For the children, both types of cart were great diversions. In her memoirs, Elizabeth Akers Allen writes, "We chased the dripping ice wagon and scooped up fragments of ice chipped from large blocks which were lifted with ice tongs and carried into people's houses for their refrigeration. Sometimes I would be permitted to fill a dishpan half full of these fragments and Mama would roll the lemons and make lemonade."[9]

Photo courtesy of the Bar Harbor Historical Society

BEFORE THE CIVIL WAR, people primarily drank coffee, tea, or alcoholic beverages because, without refrigeration, it was difficult to preserve milk. Those who owned a cow had fresh milk for drinking, as cottager Prall Grant Bacon describes: "Milk was not a problem as all the natives had cows. But it was a subject of uncertainty. Mr. Higgins was our dairyman and many times, supper would be ready, awaiting the arrival of the milk. The maid would appear to announce that Mr. Higgins's cow was lost in the woods and there would be no milk that evening. The musical tinkles of the cow bells wafted through the woods, accompanying all the hikers."[10] As Bar Harbor's social status rose, so, too, did the consumption of milk. Dairy farm owners on the island increased their production and began delivering the milk in picturesque wagons such as this one, driven by Henry Sweet.

Photo courtesy of the Sargent Family

THIS EARLY PHOTO shows Bar Harbor's first firehouse, designed for the Fountain Rodick Engine Company #1. Named for one of its founding members, the company organized in 1877, but it was not until a catastrophic event in 1881 that this engine house was built. The founding members had gathered to elect officers when a fire erupted at the year-old St. Sauveur Hotel on Mount Desert Street. Within an hour, the structure was ruined, despite heroic efforts by the volunteer firemen. Soon after, the company finished their interrupted business and elected the following officers: E. J. Winship, S. H. and F. Rodick, J. W. Manchester, A. L. and B. S. Higgins, C. Ingalls, C. DeLaittre, and H. P. Hapworth.

A year later, the company had a new home for its Bar Harbor Hose Company #1 and W. M. Roberts Hook and Ladder Co. Today's firehouse, designed by Fred Savage, dates back to 1910 and incorporates a loud siren to summon the firefighters.

Photo courtesy of the Maine Historic Preservation Commission

As THIS FIRE at the Graves Brothers' livery on November 24, 1901, illustrates, flames could destroy a building quickly despite the valiant efforts of sixteen firemen. At this time, buildings and houses were built primarily of wood, heated with coal or wood, and illuminated with kerosene or gas. All of these elements combined to produce a highly flammable environment. The firefighters had horse-drawn equipment, and only a slim possibility of finding a water source nearby because there were so few hydrants. At times, all they could do was try to prevent the fire from spreading to other buildings.

Rituals and traditions developed around the company, and the annual Firemen's Ball was one of them. Proceeds from the gala event supported the firehouse. "In one case the annual ball, held in the fall of 1896, brought in $585.80. With expenses of only $110.19, the department realized a tidy profit."[11]

Photo courtesy of the Bar Harbor Fire Department

ORGANIZED IN 1884 for competitive fun as well as for fitness training, the Bar Harbor Fire Company's hose-reel running team once achieved the second-best time in the state. The Orioles, as they were called, were in Ellsworth on this day, commemorating their success in a race. Speed, strength, and skill were key to winning the events, in which teams connected specific lengths of hose to an engine and pumped a certain amount of water. The tasks were timed and the fastest group won. Each member of the eighteen-man team was assigned a specific task, such as coupling the nozzle or leading the hose. Often the races were held as part of Fourth of July celebrations, but in Bar Harbor, the team also demonstrated their prowess and agility for the horse show crowd.

Photo courtesy of the Maine Historic Preservation Commission

EDEN SCHOOLCHILDREN, like this group of thirty-seven pupils posing with their teacher (c. 1890), did not spend much time attending classes. Their school year was arranged around agricultural seasons and consisted of two nine-week terms, one in the winter and one in the summer. An extra term was available for those who would go on to high school.

It's easy to imagine these scholars daydreaming of their free weeks between school terms, especially as spring approached. May Day was one of the annual highlights for a child, according to A. L. Higgins: "This event signified the end of winter when they could shed the copper-toed boots and stockings and run, race, 'drive hoop,' and frolic through the numerous old fields."

The growth of the student body in the Eden township—from 463 scholars in 1870 to 712 two decades later—meant building new schools and hiring more teachers. Male teachers generally taught the winter term and earned an average wage in the 1890s of $55.75 per month, not including their board costs. Female teachers, usually unmarried, could expect less than half that amount per month for teaching the summer term.

Photo courtesy of the Bar Harbor Historical Society

Local Pastimes

WHEN THE SUMMER COLONY left for their winter homes, Bar Harbor's permanent residents could relax and have the mountains, lakes, paths, and streams all to themselves. Island men frequently took this time to head to the forests and shores on fall hunting expeditions, sometimes traveling to camps on the mainland to hunt deer, moose, and small game, producing a winter feast for family and friends.

On a crisp fall day in October 1894, this group of villagers—(from left to right) William Sherman, Martin Pendleton, John Roberts, F. T. Young, W. B. Higgins, A. L. Higgins, and Charles Conners—left early in the morning to hunt sea ducks. They took a boat to Turtle Island, located between Schooner Head and Schoodic Point. Dressed in tall leather boots and warm sweaters, and armed with shotguns, these seven brought down 250 coots in just a few hours. Such an unusually successful trip warranted a photograph.

Photo courtesy of the Bar Harbor Historical Society

AROUND BAR HARBOR, ample opportunities could be found for a rewarding fishing expedition, as this family's catch shows. Anglers could head to the Atlantic to wrestle with cod or sea bass, or they could hike down to Eagle Lake where plenty of speckled trout and salmon awaited the sportsman. With more than a dozen lakes and streams on the island, there was no shortage of fishing spots. After locals stocked Eagle Lake with more than 20,000 young salmon fry in 1886, fishermen were hooking salmon that tipped the scale at six pounds apiece. The sportsmen's families turned the bounty into many delicious lunches and dinners. In a typical workman's lunch of the day, one would find home-cured stripped fish, some soda biscuits, and a jar of stewed tea.

Photo courtesy of the Maine Historic Preservation Commission

THIRTY GOOD-HUMORED FRIENDS gather to escort the newly married Louise Newman and George Berry to the wharf to begin their honeymoon in February 1913. Archie Getchell (at far left) led the procession, with doleful music provided by drummer John Wescott and trombonist Edward Smith. Men and women carried suitcases and long boxes conspicuously labeled I BELONG TO THE WEDDING PARTY, just in case people wondered who these well-dressed partiers might be. Like many villagers, Berry and his wife had a close-knit community of friends. Louise had grown up in the village. Berry, who was president of the First National Bank of Bar Harbor, was a newcomer—"from away," as they say. Despite this low status, his involvement in several fraternal orders and clubs soon won him many friends who were happy to enjoy a good prank at his expense.

Photo courtesy of the Bar Harbor Historical Society

SO MUCH SNOW fell on Bar Harbor in 1923 that these industrious men and boys had to dig a tunnel through ten-foot snowdrifts to reach the doors beyond. Children undoubtedly enjoyed the winter abundance more than their elders did. "Cold weather never bothered me," claimed Elizabeth Akers Allen in her memoirs. "I pulled men's boot socks over my shoes or rubbers, then climbed to the second-floor ramp of the Davis Buckboard Company building on School Street and jumped into the deep drifts below."[1]

When children got sick, however, it was no fun at all. Local resident Claire Lambert described how children with communicable diseases would be sent to the "Pest House," a small cabin in the woods on the Eagle Lake Road, where they could recover without endangering others. Though there was a hospital in town, built in 1899, it mostly served the summer people until World War II.

Photo courtesy of Raymond Strout

"COASTING [SLEDDING] on the steep hills of Mt. Kebo golf links find frozen snow as smooth as varnish and slipping over the hilltop for the descent with terrific express train speed is a good deal like gliding over the brink of Niagara," wrote a *Bar Harbor Times* correspondent.[2] Club membership requirements did not prevent the locals from using the Kebo Valley Club hills as their own winter wonderland.

When the town organized a winter carnival, skiing and sledding competitions attracted both young and old. Some children tried their first Eskimo Pie there, a novelty for the times. The carnival continued until the 1960s, but with each year the number of participants dropped as the popularity of indoor amusements grew.

Photo courtesy of Raymond Strout

THE SIX-HUNDRED-FOOT Eagle Lake toboggan slide, built by volunteers in 1922, was the longest and steepest in the state. It offered an exciting ride to those who dared make the trip to the ice below. The ride was free, but local Benny Hawkes levied some sweat-equity for each trip. Everyone who wanted a run was required to haul a bucket of water to the top and dowse the track to keep it iced. The toboggan chute only lasted two years, though it persisted much longer in the memories of those who dared to take the remarkable ride.

A decade later, Eagle Lake became the location for another daring pastime when an entrepreneur gave rides in his ski plane for a penny a pound. For Florence Ames, the fee rate turned to her advantage. "They always guessed my weight wrong!" exclaimed Mrs. Ames, "so I was charged for less than I weighed. The trip thrilled me to death."

Photo courtesy of Raymond Strout

ICE-BOATING on the lakes and bays of the island could become an addicting sport for speed-seekers willing to brave the cold temperatures. These iceboats, poised on Eagle Lake, were ready for racers. In February 1883, a newspaper correspondent gathered the courage to try the sport, signing on with young Chelsea Hodgkins. As soon as Santiago, the writer, was settled amidships, the boy trimmed in and they were off like blue lightning across frozen Frenchman Bay. "I had my hands full trying to hold on . . . I kept wondering if my companion had been a regular and earnest worker in the Sunday school." Despite his fears, Santiago concluded, "Such exhilarating rapture and wild glad feeling of perfect abandon I never before experienced—balloons, mules, velocipedes [bicycles], handcarts, nitro-glycerine and all other modes of quick transit may go to thunder—I want an ice-boat."[3]

Photo courtesy of Alison Salsbury

THIS GROUP of local men and women are about to take off for a row across the glassy sapphire waters of Eagle Lake during their time off from work. Particularly in the summers, the life of cottage staff revolved around their employer's schedule. "We had a day off, if you could call it a day . . . we still had to do our work in the morning," explained Adelaide Cousins, a chambermaid for the Potter Palmer family. Even after she was married, Cousins lived at the estate for the season. In the mornings, she would help the parlor maid clean the front rooms, and then proceed to tidy the bedrooms. She might finish her workday in the early afternoon, or continue on until evening, if the family had company. Though the hours could be long, Cousins was pleased with her situation. "The pay was $16 per week with room, board and uniforms. I thought I was wealthy."[4]

Photo courtesy of Alison Salsbury

Veterans of the James M. Parker Post, Grand Army of the Republic, gathered around Bar Harbor's Civil War Monument in 1911. This monument, dedicated in November 1897, served as a reminder of Eden's soldiers who had fought to maintain the Union. N. H. Higgins of Ellsworth designed the statue with symbols of the four branches of service, one on each side of the granite column. The quarry on nearby Deer Isle provided the granite base.

Eighteen of Eden's sons joined the 1st Maine Heavy Artillery unit, a regiment whose heroism is revered in history. Willard Fogg told of the day in 1864, during the siege of Petersburg, when his regiment was called to serve as a regular infantry unit and charged the Confederate fortifications: "The boys from Maine sustained the greatest loss of any regiment in one action of the war. Over 635 men were killed and wounded out of 900 engaged, a loss of over 70 percent in less than seven minutes."[5]

Photo courtesy of the Bar Harbor Historical Society

STRIKING HER BEST Annie Oakley pose, Annie Anthony was ready to turn her catch into dinner. In the early 1900s, Anthony lived with her husband, Frank, and son, Frank Jr., at the Satterlee estate, where Frank Sr. was the gardener. Mrs. Anthony worked in town at the music store. When winter arrived and traveling to town became difficult, Mrs. Anthony and her son stayed in the village on weekdays. Each Friday, Mr. Anthony would collect them in the horse and buggy and take them back to their home, and then reverse that course on Sunday. This routine was not uncommon, until the advent of automobiles eased winter travel.

Photo courtesy of the Bar Harbor Historical Society

WITH THE ADVENT of improved transportation, greater prosperity, and broader educational and professional opportunities for women, Bar Harbor's ladies joined their sisters across the nation by forming the Women's Literary Club (shown here), the Women's Study Club, and the Current Events Club. Many of these local women had not attended high school and were eager to learn about the world through club activities.

The Women's Literary Club, initially known as the Reality and Fiction Club, formed in 1902 with twelve members. Despite its name, the group was devoted to the study of geography, and members took their assignments seriously. Each member selected a country to study and would then report back to the group during their weekly meetings. This costume party may have been prompted by a study of gypsies. One thing was certain: These pioneering women forged a new path for their daughters to follow.

Photo courtesy of the Bar Harbor Historical Society

AN ELABORATE European-scene backdrop provided the ambience for this play at Bar Harbor's Casino, a barn-like public hall on Cottage and Bridge streets. For more than seventy years, this simple structure, built in 1900, was the center of activity for the local people. Vaudeville performances, commencements, plays performed by local and professional talent, basketball games, wrestling matches, and lots of dances—this is where it all happened.

Every February, the hall would come alive for an entire evening with the Hayseeder's Ball, organized by the locals as a spoof on themselves. "Since the summer people seemed to think of the native population as 'hayseeds,'" explains historian Ruth Ann Hill, "the ball's participants naturally adopted full rural regalia."[6] The invitations were written on brown paper, with creative spelling, and sprinkled with hayseed. Guests spent months creating elaborate old-fashioned costumes to dance in until the wee hours.

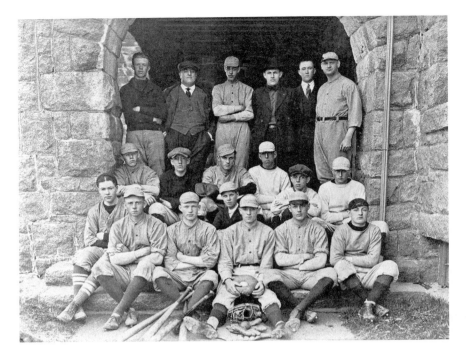

THE TRIUMPHANT 1921 Bar Harbor High School baseball team poses for a season photo. Sports, especially baseball, played an important role in island life. As early as the 1880s, Bar Harbor's community baseball team competed against other village teams in the summer. Though Bar Harbor would host a short-lived semiprofessional baseball league, it was the high school and pickup games that survived through the years.

Cottagers John Kennedy, Morris Jesup, and George Bowdoin worked with local real estate broker Edward Mears to establish a YMCA building on Mount Desert Street in 1899. Built with timbers from the razed Grand Central Hotel, the Y soon became the hub of athletics, from basketball and hardball games, to bowling and, later, swimming. By 1930, the Y served more than three hundred boys and men, and a new building (which was replaced by the present Abbe Museum) provided expanded facilities to meet the growing needs of the community.

Photo courtesy of the Jesup Memorial Library

THESE ATHLETIC Bar Harbor teenagers are ready to play ball. Mrs. John S. Kennedy donated funds to build a YWCA building, completed in 1913, where girls could play ball, socialize, and develop good Christian morals. Female high school students could stay at the YWCA if their homes were too far away for daily travel. Women could also board there while working for cottagers or businesses during the busy summers. Today, the YWCA (at far right on facing page) continues to offer long-term accommodations, as well as social and fitness programs for women.

Photo courtesy of the Bar Harbor Historical Society

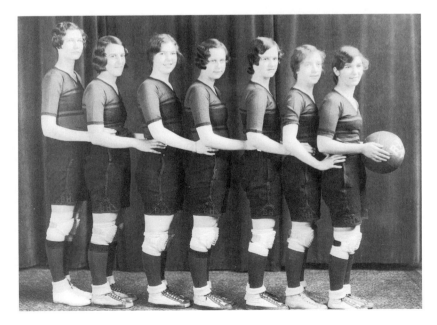

WHAT BEGAN IN 1875 as a small private collection of books, owned by Bar Harbor's summer visitors and shared with the year-round residents, blossomed over time into the Jesup Memorial Library, named in memory of New Yorker Morris K. Jesup. New York architects William Adams Delano and Chester Holmes Aldrich designed this 1911 Colonial Revival building for Bar Harbor, not only to house books, but also to bring the community together for exhibits and meetings. At the building's dedication, the Honorable L. B. Deasy explained, "It is books that bring to and lay at the feet of each new century all the worthwhile wealth of past centuries . . . a gift of books and of the means of preserving them and of distributing them and of stimulating the use of more and better books is the best and most perfect public gift." With an endowment of $50,000, Mrs. Jesup not only perpetuated the memory of her husband's generous nature, but also fostered the enjoyment of books for generations to come.

Photo courtesy of the Maine Historic Preservation Commission

Changing Times

MINISTER AND WRITER Benjamin de Costa described a hike not far from this spot in 1871: "We were on top of . . . Dry [Dorr] Mountain, picking blueberries and seeking for the best way across the ravine which separated us from Green [Cadillac]. We finally decided to take the most shallow part of the ravine and push straight across. . . . at every step we were in danger of dislodging huge masses of rock that needed scarcely more than a finger's touch to send them thundering below."[1]

This group of hikers traversing the Cadillac Trail many years later could do so confidently because of the diligence and hard work of volunteer trail builders. Some, like Waldron Bates, took great pride in rearranging the terrain to allow the hiker a dramatic perspective. Hikers continue to benefit from the path maker's thigh-strengthening handiwork and foresight.

Photo courtesy of Raymond Strout

Summer residents created Village Improvement Associations in the 1890s to raise the sanitation and aesthetic standards of their adopted communities. Representing the four island VIA Path Committees were: (from left) Joseph Allen (Seal Harbor), Walter Buell (Southwest Harbor), Fred Weeks (Bar Harbor), Professor Grandgent (SWH), William Turner (Northeast Harbor), Thomas McIntire (SH), and George B. Dorr (BH). Their philosophy in creating new paths was to "open up new avenues of access to the beautiful hills and lakes, and to the grand outlooks, which make the island of Mount Desert one of the most picturesque spots on the face of the globe."[2]

The island's original paths were created by Native Americans and then used by early settlers. In the 1890s rusticators built or improved more than 125 paths in a burst of trail making led by summer residents Herbert Jaques, Waldron Bates, Edward Rand, Rudolph Brunnow, and George Dorr.

Photo courtesy of Raymond Strout

Charles W. Eliot (in dark blazer), president of Harvard University, watches as three young children helped plant a tree. Both Eliot and his friend, George B. Dorr (at right), can be credited with creating Acadia National Park, which began in 1901 as a charitable land trust known as the Hancock County Trustees of Public Reservations. Eliot and his son, a landscape architect, recognized that the island's summits had just barely escaped being developed as sites for more hotels such as the former Green Mountain House. Future developments were inevitable unless the land was protected. Summer people from Bar Harbor, Seal Harbor, and Northeast Harbor contributed land, beginning with the area around the Beehive and the Bowl, donated by Mrs. Charles Homan in 1908.

Photo courtesy of the Abbe Museum, Bar Harbor, Maine

CANOEING AROUND his placid pond, New York surgeon Dr. Robert Abbe explained his zest for life: "Conquest only comes from persistent climbing upward. Often it seems like the excitement I have felt when climbing Sargent or Green [Cadillac] Mountain . . . [is because] the nearer one gets to the top, the harder it seems—then all of a sudden one gets there. That glorious experience I have had many, many times in every field of adventure, in surgery, science or climbing, and I like the game." His enthusiasm led him to invent new techniques for plastic surgery and radiation treatments for cancer, and to establish a museum for Native American antiquities in Bar Harbor. Abbe often claimed that he would spend nine months of the year in New York dreaming about the three months he would spend on Mount Desert Island. In 1898 he bought the Brook End cottage near Duck Brook, where he could often be found rowing around this pond with his two black swans, Pierre and Marie, named for his colleagues, the Curies, discoverers of radium.

Photo courtesy of the Abbe Museum, Bar Harbor, Maine

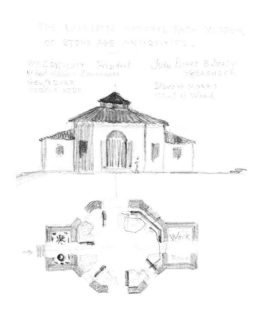

ROBERT ABBE's fascination with archaeology led him to buy a local collection of ancient Native American tools discovered in shell heaps around Frenchman Bay. Over time he purchased other artifacts, not to amass an inventory for personal enjoyment, but to preserve and share that heritage with others. At a time when the world was experiencing rapid growth in technology, Abbe wanted to create a place where visitors could appreciate the prehistoric past of the Native Americans. With the help of friends Eliot and Dorr, Abbe organized a private museum in 1926.

Abbe's drawing talent can be seen in this sketch he made for the original museum building. Built in 1928, the modest Abbe Museum was located trailside near the base of Dorr Mountain. Though Abbe would not live to see his museum inaugurated, his dream was realized. At its new downtown location in the village of Bar Harbor, Abbe's collection continues to educate island visitors about Native American culture.

Photo courtesy of the Abbe Museum, Bar Harbor, Maine

CHILDREN FROM Bar Harbor's St. Joseph's School are shown here at the picturesque Sieur de Monts Spring, near the site of the original Abbe Museum. George Dorr is credited with having the vision to preserve this spring. In the early 1900s, a commercial water-bottling company owned and tapped this freshwater resource. With only minutes to spare before another commercial group was set to purchase the spring, Dorr bought it for $5,000 in 1909. By placing the property under the auspices of the Hancock County Trustees of Public Reservations, Dorr ensured its protection from future commercial interests. Local architect Fred Savage was hired to build a picturesque gazebo over the spring, based on a classical design by Egisto Fabbri.

Photo courtesy of the William Otis Sawtelle Collections, Acadia National Park

IN MEMORY of her husband, John Jacob Astor's great-grandson, Mrs. John Innes Kane (at right) donated funds to create a path in the Gorge, along the Little Meadows. In 1915, when this photo was taken, some summer residents, such as Mrs. Kane and her sister Mrs. Bridgham (left), were still summering at Bar Harbor, though many of their friends had died or left for other resorts. William Jay Schieffelin Jr. wrote in his memoir that Bar Harbor had become too pretentious and overcrowded, so he and others had simply moved to more secluded spots.

With the protectors of old traditions passing away or leaving, Bar Harbor started to change. The pace of life quickened with the acceptance of automobiles, and the resort began to see a rise in day-trippers even as long-term cottagers left to visit other resorts. When the federal government levied an income tax in 1913, rusticators had less money to maintain the cottages and their large staffs. Despite these changes, the remaining cottagers still enjoyed a whirl of club and social activities, both on land and on water.

Photo courtesy of Raymond Strout

Once the United States entered World War I, displays of patriotism were common. As this procession of army and navy servicemen marched down Main Street in Bar Harbor, shipments of supplies prepared by local Red Cross volunteers were already headed overseas. Spurred by reports of shortages in the field hospitals, Red Cross volunteers met frequently at the Jesup Memorial Library print room to cut and wrap gauze bandages, sew pajamas and convalescent robes, and knit garments for the soldiers. Knitting needles clicked furiously, and within a month, volunteers had transformed more than two hundred pounds of yarn into sweaters and socks. One islander admitted that she thought the sweaters were dreadful, and she pitied the poor souls who would have to wear them.

Even the youngest citizens found creative ways to help. George Cleaves, age seven, gathered the hotel arrival information for the *Bar Harbor Life* newspaper and asked for his pay in Thrift Stamps, a "baby bond." As the newspaper editor reported, "He [Cleaves] acknowledges his commissions with a military salute and performs his duties like a major."[3]

Photo courtesy of the James M. Parker Post, American Legion

Like many of his fellow gentry, Alessandro Fabbri (at center) was too old for active duty during the war. Instead, he offered his services as an amateur radio enthusiast—as well as his highly powerful radio transmitter—to the government. Though it took some convincing, the navy commissioned Fabbri in 1917 as an ensign in the Naval Coast Reserve, assigning him to supervise the construction of the Transatlantic Radio Station at Otter Cliffs. Within a year, more than two hundred men were handling some twenty thousand messages daily from overseas.

"When you think that the origin of this energy," Fabbri reported, "is thousands of miles away, being transmitted by etheric vibrations, it is truly amazing."[4] In recognition of his work at the Station, the navy awarded Fabbri a Navy Cross in 1920.

In this photograph he stood in a dark suit with some of the local servicemen, including Gerald Alley, Pearl McFarland, Vernon McQuinn, Forest Norwood, Herman Leland, Jalbert Stevens, and cottager Gardiner Sherman in the straw boater.

Photo courtesy of the James M. Parker Post, American Legion

THE KEBO VALLEY CLUB's three-level putting greens, the only ones of their kind in the country, offered an abundance of activity, especially after women were allowed on the links. For years, putting contests, accompanied by fashionable afternoon teas and cocktail parties, were regular Monday-afternoon events at Kebo. By the Depression years, however, the Bar Harbor Club had replaced Kebo Valley Club as the center of social activity. By 1938, service at Kebo had been cut in half, and the last tennis courts were dismantled. Throughout the World War II years, Kebo tottered on with only two groundskeepers, despite boasting members with names like Ford and Rocke-feller. Then, just as the war subsided and things started to look up, all hopes were dashed when Kebo went up in flames in the fire of 1947. The only relics saved were the Wright and Bates tournament cups.

The Kebo Valley Club was later rebuilt, and lives strong to this day, open for all to enjoy—one of the most beautiful golf courses in the country.

Photo courtesy of the Bar Harbor Historical Society

152

New Yorker Agnes Carpenter understood what her city friends needed once they arrived for a visit on the island: fresh air and good food. Agnes loved the outdoors, and with her mother, Mrs. Miles Carpenter, had created a labyrinth of gardens on their Hauterive estate, providing a variety of outdoor summer parlors.

When the eminent internist S. Whittington Gorham arrived with his wife, Elizabeth, for a visit in 1928, Agnes arranged a morning breakfast for them by the balustrade. She had the servants transfer all of the major elements of the breakfast room to this outdoor spot: rug, table, linens, china, bouquets of flowers, and even the birds for company.

While some picnics went to this extreme of formality, others were more modest, and involved packing a simple sandwich for lunch at the summit, overlooking the mountains and sea.

Photo courtesy of the Bar Harbor Historical Society

THE ROARING TWENTIES had arrived, and rising industries had produced new millionaires seeking a summer resort. Prominent names such as Rockefeller, Ford, Stotesbury, and radio pioneer Atwater Kent joined the list of cottagers at the island's resorts. On a fine crystalline day in 1920, when this picture was taken, Seal Harbor residents John D. and Abby Rockefeller brought her Aldrich siblings and cousins for a visit with Agnes Carpenter at Hauterive.

Though the cottagers' names may have changed over time, the vibrant social network of an exclusive resort remained the same. On the international level, Bar Harbor could boast more foreign ministers than its competing resort, Newport. Foreign diplomats would move their entire embassy to the cool environs of Bar Harbor for the summer to socialize, hike, and play golf with prominent Americans.

Photo courtesy of the Bar Harbor Historical Society

ROOSEVELT'S CIVILIAN CONSERVATION CORPS (CCC), a New Deal program, offered young men an opportunity for vocational training and employment, two scarce commodities in the 1930s. More than two hundred boys lived at the CCC camp on McFarland Hill, and Linwood Robshaw was one of them. During the winter, he recalls, "It was cold. But most of the boys in the CCC camp never complained. At the time we all felt lucky that we had a good place to sleep and three meals a day and something to do."[5] The boys' families welcomed their monthly salaries of $30. Crews were kept busy throughout the year building cabins (as shown), comfort stations, paths, directional signs, and other projects to improve Acadia National Park. Simultaneously, John D. Rockefeller Jr. was financing crews to build carriage and motor roads and paths. By the end of the 1930s, the public and private efforts had propped up the local economy while creating over 260 miles of paths and roads.

Photo courtesy of the William Otis Sawtelle Collections, Acadia National Park

THESE WORKERS APPRECIATED the CCC jobs. "Behind the bank there were many houses," noted villager Elizabeth Gorer, "and one of those, a tiny house, belonged to a tailor. With no heat and the house right on the ground with no basement, the kids who lived there would come up to our house to get warm. At that same time, there was a store downtown that sold only silk underwear." The distinction between such poverty and wealth startled Gorer. During the summer, Main Street was still lined with expensive Packards, Pierce-Arrows, and Rolls-Royces driven by well-turned-out chauffeurs. In earlier days, bouquets of colorful flowers had perfumed the homes of both locals and summer people, but as the economy soured, this custom faded, leading to the closing of most local florist shops and their associated greenhouses.

Photo courtesy of the William Otis Sawtelle Collections, Acadia National Park

TWO HOLSTEIN STEERS pulled the sled as two farmers at McFarland's Farm collected rocks from the plowed field. In the 1930s and '40s, farming continued on the island, even though the demand for fresh vegetables waned with reduced summer domestic staffs and shorter vacations. Some cottagers, such as the Satterlees, employed full-time gardeners who grew potatoes, beets, carrots, and watercress that were then shipped to their winter home in Delaware. During World War II, citizens were encouraged to grow their own food in Victory Gardens. Rising to the challenge, villagers in Bar Harbor grew their own food and canned it in the Casino, a makeshift community canning center. It was a tough environment for farmers, but they were still making a living at it through the Depression. In 1915, an A&P grocery store opened in Bar Harbor. During the 1940s, it and other chain stores dealt a final blow to small farms on the island.

Photo courtesy of the William Otis Sawtelle Collections, Acadia National Park

"DRINK YOUR MILK—it's good for you!" was heard by many children as America recognized this beverage as a near-perfect food. Convenient morning deliveries, right to the doorstep, were made possible thanks to dairy farmers such as Percy Kief (at right) and his young assistant, who delivered quarts of milk in sturdy glass bottles for ten cents each. At one point, more than forty dairy farms, each with an average of sixteen to twenty cows, produced milk for the local and tourist markets.

Spurred by the demand for pasteurized milk, Kief joined with some of the other local dairymen, including Frank Andrews, Henry Sweet, Clarence Alley, George Fogg, and William DeLaittre, to establish the Mount Desert Island Dairies, a cooperative with a pasteurizing plant on Main Street in Bar Harbor. Despite this measure, they couldn't fight the changing times. Improved milk-processing systems and big-chain grocery stores closed down the small farms by the 1950s, which meant an end to the milkman's morning greetings.

Photo courtesy of John Clark

PATRONS FLOCK TO the Criterion Theater in 1937. The elegant, white-haired owner, George McKay, spared no expense on this project, creating a ritzy ambience with velvet seats and an art-deco decor.

After cocktails and a refined dinner, young aristocrats attired in dinner jackets and long dresses would arrive in chauffeured autos. They would be promptly seated in the mezzanine section, while the locals sat downstairs. George McKay Jr., the owner's son, described the difficulties of this arrangement: "You had to be careful [about] which summer person you [seated] with which summer person. You know, they're kind of cliquey. There were people who thought they should have been millionaires, but weren't, who always tried to get in with the millionaires."

By the 1950s, jackets and long dresses were no longer donned for movie nights at the Criterion, and the advent of television further shrank the size of the audience. Nonetheless, the theater's placement on the National Register of Historic Places asserted its architectural significance.

Photo courtesy of the Salt Institute for Documentary Studies, Portland, Maine

IN JUNE 1921, a group of scientists moved their Harpswell Laboratory facilities from southern Maine to this Salisbury Cove location and renamed it the Mount Desert Island Biological Laboratory (MDIBL). This cove had been the site of Benjamin Emery's shipyard, where schooners were built and launched in the 1800s. The Wild Gardens of Acadia, a land-holding company founded by George Dorr and John D. Rockefeller Jr., donated the Emery property for the MDIBL. Scientists would move there for the summer months, families in tow, to study marine animal and plant structures. Except for a brief closure during the war, the Lab continued to operate during the summers, expanding its focus to cell function. By the 1960s, the summer research staff grew to about forty-five, including many students, and later expanded to a year-round laboratory.

Photo courtesy of the Mount Desert Island Biological Laboratory

THE JACKSON LABORATORY was opened in 1929, the same year as the Bar Harbor Club, but no two institutions could have been more different. As a premier center for cancer research, the Jackson Lab created a stronger year-round community. Resort businesses or the MDI Biological Laboratory closed for the season, whereas the Jackson Lab offered a stable work environment that became vital to the island economy.

Under the leadership of Dr. C. C. Little (center), the Jax Lab prospered. It was said of Little that he was a friendly man, as comfortable with his secretary as he was with a visiting dignitary, a skill that helped him raise money for the Lab. After the 1947 fire obliterated the facility, Dr. Little wasted no time in rebuilding what would become the world's leading source of mouse strains for biomedical research of all types, expanding beyond their initial focus on cancer research.

Photo courtesy of the Jackson Laboratory Archives

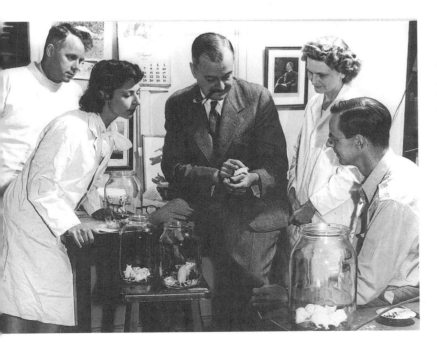

DENTIST, BANK PRESIDENT, and town legend, Dr. John B. Ells (at right) was a significant Bar Harbor persona. From the 1940s through the 1960s, he was responsible for bringing American, English, and French warships to the harbor, most notably the USS *Missouri* in 1945. Ells's lifelong passion for warships began during the Gilded Age, when naval boats visited the harbor each August during Squadron Week. He could be found at the town pier on summer afternoons—dressed in white flannel pants, a blue blazer, two-toned shoes, a straw hat, and with a cigar in hand—welcoming people to his town and encouraging them to see the warships. He made sure that the servicemen from the ships were entertained. His collection of plaques from ship captains demonstrated how much the servicemen appreciated Bar Harbor's ambassador.

Photo courtesy of the Bar Harbor Historical Society

HERE, A YOUNG Sargent and Ellie Collier can be seen inquiring about the wartime scenery under the watchful eye of their father's lens. During World War II the navy used this airfield (now the Hancock County – Bar Harbor Airport) for its observation planes, and commandeered the old Reading Room from the Bar Harbor Yacht Club as its headquarters.

Everything from gas, silk stockings, coffee, and cream to meat, peas, butter, sugar, and so forth, was rationed, and shortages were the norm, even for such things as diapers. Undeterred, the villagers continued to ask how they could help the war effort. By 1943, more than five hundred of them had volunteered for the Civilian Defense Corps, to keep watch for enemy war planes and submarines. At the end of the war, the soldiers returned home but life on the island would never be the same.

Photo by Sargent F. Collier, courtesy of the Collier family

As FIRE CHIEF David Sleeper polished his truck for this photograph, little did he suspect that an overwhelming disaster was imminent. On October 17, 1947, a small dump fire started to spread, and in seven days, it would burn more than 18,000 acres.

Claire Lambert remembered evacuating with a cedar chest packed with clothes and yarn. "Why yarn, I don't know," she said. One of her family members carried a satchel full of money. As they drove out of town, everything around them was burning. "We never panicked," she explained. "We figured that we could always get into the ocean."

The Goldthwait family, including six-year-old John, evacuated to Cranberry Island. "The sky was filled with smoke in horizontal wisps," he recalled, "and, of course, we packed impractical things." He remembered looking out his Cranberry Island bedroom window and seeing all of Mount Desert Island glowing like red embers.

Photo courtesy of the Bar Harbor Historical Society

AT THE CORNER of Eden and West streets, a member of the National Guard patrols near the site of the demolished DeGregoire Hotel. A pivotal stand in the fire, it was here that the flames switched direction due to a shift in the wind, just barely missing the town center. The once-beautiful neighborhood along this avenue was reduced to ashes and rubble.

The fire was capricious, leaving some buildings standing, while others next door were reduced to ashes. At the Fenno estate, the garage and fence burned, but the cottage was spared. In the aftermath of the fire, Bar Harbor's many architectural fragments and treasures became prime sites for looters. The few ruins that still remain today offer a glimpse of Bar Harbor's romantic past.

Photo courtesy of the Mildred McCormick Estate

The forest fire that swept through Bar Harbor in October of 1947 was propelled by eighty-mile-per-hour winds. President Truman proclaimed the island a disaster area, and the Parisian newspaper *Le Figaro*, cried that Bar Harbor had been set ablaze by Maine "peasants" protesting the great landed aristocracy, when, in fact, many of the loyal gardeners had saved their employers' homes by wetting down roofs until the flames forced them away. Some houses, such as Highseas along Schooner Head Road and Miss Mildred McCormick's farm on Eden Street, were saved by brave caretakers. Other estate owners could thank dedicated Coast Guardsmen for the survival of their cottages. Despite these valiant efforts, 170 year-round houses, 67 summer cottages, and 5 hotels burned in the fire.

Photo courtesy of the *Bangor Daily News*

Even as the fire encroached on the outskirts of the village, these telephone operators remained at their stations. Standing left to right are Minnie Allen, Ruth Higgins, Charlotte Stewart, Elizabeth Alley, Florence Ames, Pauline Johnson, Hattie Mosley, Hazel Megquire, Pauline Nolen, Chris Cowan, Thelma Davis, Lillian Wiley, and Ruth Liscomb.

Mrs. Ames recalled the scene: "People were very calm, even as word came in that the Kebo Valley Club and Forest Avenue were burning." With four children to support, Mr. and Mrs. Ames found what jobs they could after the fire. He was the foreman at the Bar Harbor Beverage Company, and she worked for the Jackson Lab and the water company. "My husband and I practically never saw each other, but we got through." There wasn't much else to do but forge ahead.

Photo courtesy of Florence Ames

MANY ISLANDERS had not only lost
their homes and belongings in the fire,
but their jobs as well. This crisis mo-
bilized many into action to help their
beloved town, including (from left to
right) Dr. Margaret Dyer, Florence
Rodick, Mary Graham, Mrs. Ambrose
Higgins, and Mrs. Edward Browning Jr.
This group of permanent and summer
residents organized Bar Harbor Handi-
crafts, to bring recreation and income
to the people of Mount Desert Island.
About 75 to 100 island women made
household goods and clothing, such as
aprons, quilts, and rugs, to be sold at
the weeklong sale held every July at the
Jesup Memorial Library. Not only did
Mrs. Browning, Mrs. Sargent Collier,
and others suggest specific products to
make, they also encouraged their friends
to buy goods at the sale. Their marketing was so successful that after the sale
closed one year, salespersons sent pack-
ages to more than thirty-six states.

Photo courtesy of Mrs. Stockton Andrews

As the summer colony dwindled after the Depression, locals sought ways to bolster the economy. Small motels, such as these Wee Eden cottages, attracted vacationers who were on a budget. With Acadia National Park just minutes away, these modest accommodations became very popular.

This scale of housing, however, would not suit aristocratic fiction writer Mary Roberts Rinehart. Though her estate had burned in the fire, she still wanted to continue her Bar Harbor summer tradition. Fortunately, the Bar Harbor townspeople built the Bar Harbor Motor Inn, incorporating the old Bar Harbor Reading Room. Though smaller than their former summer cottages, this new hotel provided a place where Mrs. Rinehart and her friend Mrs. Rothschild could feel at home, assisted by their personal help and still wearing their pearls.

Photo courtesy of the Maine Historic Preservation Commission

The Stotesbury family's abandoned Wingwood had seen better days by the 1950s, when this photo was taken. The same held true for other behemoths such as the Turrets, the Breakers, Corfield, and Baymeath. The next generation could no longer afford these relics of an earlier lifestyle. Cottagers complained of exorbitant taxes and the high operating costs of these white elephants. Joseph Pulitzer Jr. calculated that at the peak of its use in the 1920s and '30s, four months residence at Chatwold cost him between $20,000 and $30,000 annually. If left unoccupied, the property still cost him around $9,000. No renters could be found.

Some families, such the Thorndikes and Pulitzers, chose to tear down their summer cottages; others abandoned the old estates, while still others waited it out and sighed with relief when the fire swept away the outdated mansions. As Joseph Pulitzer Jr. commented in 1942, "[T]he day of the summer palace is over."[6]

Photo courtesy of James Blanchard

By the 1950s, when this view of Main Street was taken, Bar Harbor residents had been experiencing declining incomes for more than twenty years. The trouble began with the Depression, and was further exacerbated by the changing lifestyles of the cottagers, around which the economy had revolved for decades. The year-round community had been talking about what kind of changes were needed since the 1930s, but with few results. The 1947 fire became a catalyst. Immediately after the disaster, the Jackson Lab and the Kebo Valley Club began rebuilding, and the national park planted new trees all over the scarred hillsides and valleys.

The fire also gave the Bar Harbor Planning Commission the momentum it needed to carry out plans it had been working on for years: First, the town purchased the wharf area property and built the Bar Harbor Motor Inn; then, they built a terminal for Canada's *Bluenose* ferry; and finally, they created a park near the wharf. R. Amory Thorndike, a former rusticator turned permanent resident, was a leader in these endeavors, along with villagers Seth Libby, Leslie Brewer, and others.

"Certainly the community is not dead, or dying. If it has scars, it wears them with dignity, even cheerfulness," asserted Mary Roberts Rinehart.[7]

Photo courtesy of the Bar Harbor Historical Society

Majorettes lead a band down Cottage Street in the 1950s. Parades like this one brought spectators out on Memorial Day, the Fourth of July, and Labor Day. Smaller incomes did not prevent islanders from continuing to enjoy their social clubs and fraternal orders, even though the membership numbers had declined.

During this era, mothers and fathers gathered for bridge parties while their children's lives revolved around school, church groups, scouting, and socials at the Ys. During warm summer afternoons, one could always find a good-sized crowd gathered at the athletic field, ready to cheer on the local baseball team. Club memberships were becoming more democratic. The Women's Literary Society's membership dropped the practice of blackballing, and local villagers were finally allowed to become members of the Kebo Valley Club.

Photo courtesy of the Bar Harbor Historical Society

John Wall, grandson of Butterfield's founder, remembered the day of the fire. "In that one day, we lost 99 percent of our business because our customers were almost all cottagers." Not willing to be defeated, the Wall family began selling sandwiches and other take-out foods, and continued filling orders for cottagers in the other island resorts. Capitalizing on visitors' love of Maine's balsam firs, they began making holiday wreaths, and soon were sending out more than 1,800 of these fragrant items to customers throughout the U.S.

Butterfield's joins Sherman's Books and Stationery, the West End Pharmacy, and Bee's as enterprises that have lasted more than a century, purveying a delightful mix of items geared toward local residents, summer cottagers, and the more modern tourist. Butterfield's delicious lemon cake is still a staple for any Bar Harbor picnic. Just don't ask for the recipe; it's a family secret.

Photo courtesy of John Wall

THE PARTIES AT THE Bar Harbor Club were legendary. On Tuesday and Friday nights, the summer community would descend on the club for cocktails and dinner, followed by dancing. After the fire, quiet Northeast Harbor and Seal Harbor held the largest contingent of summer residents, but the most entertaining parties were always reserved for grand old Bar Harbor. Here Patricia Scull of Northeast Harbor (right) and a friend play on rocking horses at one of the club's many theme parties.

Cottagers and their guests would have little time to rest their feet. Each of the island's private country clubs hosted dances every week. On many nights, youngsters like Potter Palmer Jr. and Oakleigh Thorne could be seen jumping off the double-decker diving board simultaneously—wearing their tuxes! Many people believed, correctly, that the Bar Harbor Club's demise was assured when the popular dances were discontinued in the early 1980s.

Photo by Sargent F. Collier, courtesy of the Collier family

BAR HARBOR BEAUTY Betty Alexander poses at the newly built Hancock County–Bar Harbor Airport, having just arrived on a flight. Beginning in 1949, the young Northwest Airlines offered regular service to the airport, located just across the bridge in Trenton.

To many, this improvement in transportation signaled a renaissance for the island's economy. The character of Bar Harbor was changing, with an increase in transient visitors and fewer exclusive shops downtown. This, combined with high taxes, spurred some summer residents to purchase moderate-sized summer homes in the neighboring resorts of Seal Harbor and Northeast Harbor. These communities had an advantage: On average, their cottages were smaller than the Bar Harbor palaces, and they had retained a cottage character throughout the decades.

Photo by Sargent F. Collier, courtesy of the Collier family

Here Mrs. Tristram Dorrance Colket, or "Fifi," daughter of Campbell's Soup president John T. Dorrance, reigned as queen of the court at a dinner dance she gave at her cottage, La Rochelle, in 1946. To Fifi's left was the bald George McMurtry, a former commander of the Lost Battalion, who was famous throughout Bar Harbor for his violent temper.

Each guest was expected to perform a song. Marshard Orchestra players held up cue cards with the lyrics to "Alexander's Ragtime Band" to aid the guests as they sang along. Around the madam's neck (at left) is the song "Me and My Shadow," by Frank Sinatra. The Colket family later donated La Rochelle to the Maine Seacoast Mission, a nondenominational organization that provides spiritual, health, and youth development programs in isolated Maine coastal and island communities.

Kebo Valley Club's Wright Cup bears the name of Mrs. Colket, who just for fun played in the 1945 golf tournament. She won, the first woman to do so, driving from the men's tees.

Photo by Sargent F. Collier, courtesy of the Collier family

Bar Harbor was famous for its extravagant "Gatsbyesque" house parties. As early as 1916, it was reported that "Bar Harbor without dancing was like Switzerland without the Alps."[8] In the 1940s, fancy champagne dinners and dances lasted well into the early morning hours. Society bands like the Marshard Orchestra and Lester Lanin Orchestra defined this era, playing the best songs for Bar Harborites and other resort-goers as well. As the end of a dance neared, bejeweled matrons would encourage the band to play on with a handsome donation.

Here at La Rochelle, the dapper "Atty" Kent, son of Atwater, is seen dancing with his elegant blonde wife, Sherri. Dancing was not the only pastime; parties at the spacious estates often featured theatrics, with guests acting in plays just as their parents and grandparents had done decades earlier.

Photo by Sargent F. Collier, courtesy of the Collier family

"THE INDESTRUCTIBLE DOWAGER of West Street still wears her jewels with grace and nobility, although the State of Maine tourmalines rather than diamonds seem to be the vogue."[9] Entirely rebuilt just before the Crash of 1929, the new Bar Harbor Club boasted ballrooms (perfect for debutante balls), dining rooms, and the large pool (shown here). The Norman-style facility was built with significant contributions from the Stotesbury and Kent patriarchs, and was a status symbol to these industrialists who themselves hardly set foot on the tennis courts or swam in the pool.

The Bar Harbor Club was, until the late 1980s, the place where Bar Harbor families went to commingle, first as summer residents, then as a stronger democratic mix of summer and year-round residents.

Photo by Sargent F. Collier, courtesy of the Collier family

THESE VACATIONERS were exploring the peace and quiet of Acadia's snow-covered terrain as they swished along on their skis. In the 1950s, the Maine government joined with the National Park Service to lure sojourners to their "Vacationland." Both the park and the surrounding area reaped the economic benefits of this new campaign, with higher numbers of visitors.

Though the miles of hiking paths had dwindled by this time to only 100, skiers could also enjoy 45 miles of carriage paths for their winter adventures. John D. Rockefeller Jr. had devoted time and money over the course of three decades to building carriage roads, motor roads, and paths throughout the park, driven by the belief that "Humans need a quiet, peaceful atmosphere; a conformation with nature."[10]

Photo courtesy of Raymond Strout

THE JORDAN POND HOUSE, an old establishment and bastion of island lore, is still the place to go for tea and popovers. Although it is located in Seal Harbor, it has always been a part of the Bar Harbor scene. The sturdy wooden structure with birch-bark paneling was a prime target for fire, and in 1979 the restaurant met a sad fate when it went up in flames. The newly rebuilt Jordan Pond House, although nowhere near as charming as the original, still feeds hordes of hungry hikers and countless numbers of local and summer families.

A new path around the pond, built over many years by dedicated Acadia Youth Conservation Corps members, offers the chance for a nice stroll before enjoying an enormous buttery popover.

Photo courtesy of Raymond Strout

SMALL IN NUMBERS, perhaps, but ahhhh, so mighty the names in the Bar Harbor's summer elite's last gasp at serious yacht racing. Luders racing began in 1947 at Bar Harbor and managed to linger for two decades or so before bringing to an end that resort's final attempt at adult sailing competition. This was it for Bar Harbor, but a good, if modest, show.

Remarkably, *Tries*, Luders #22, more than fifty years after this photo was taken, remains in the appreciative ownership of Tristram Colket Jr., who is shown here at the helm. The Milliken Luders, *North Wind*, also remains in Bar Harbor, but is nearly derelict. The *P.S.*, the Strawbridge Luders, was sold many years ago, her whereabouts now unknown. The *Anemone*, in contrast, returned in 2008 after a long hiatus in faraway states. It joined the revived fleet of Luders racing under the auspices of the Southwest Harbor Fleet.

Photo courtesy of the Bar Harbor Historical Society

THE BAR HARBOR YACHT CLUB, organized in 1885, is one of the oldest yacht clubs still in existence in America. It was housed in a variety of buildings, including quarters at the old Reading Room steel pier, the town dock, the abandoned Wingwood House, and finally, a handsome clubhouse near the Bluffs, toward Hulls Cove. Members Mrs. Oakleigh Thorne and Kenneth E. Jenkins donated the land for the new clubhouse and the pier, respectively.

A small yet loyal Bar Harbor summer clan who returned after the 1947 fire donated funds for the clubhouse and opened sailing programs for the summer and year-round youth. The young people attracted to the club—Minot Milliken, Edward Blair, and Michael Pulitzer, and others—were enjoying the "simple life" on a less-pretentious scale than what Atwater Kent had emphasized in the 1920s, and more along the lines of the Bar Harbor rusticators of yore.

Photo courtesy of the Bar Harbor Historical Society

SAM AND NANCY DUNHAM, of the Edward Browning family, relax during a midsummer escape. Bar Harbor and picnics have always been inseparable, for all inhabitants of the island. A few spots remain sacred for traditional gatherings, such as the annual Bar Harbor Yacht Club picnic at The Hop, off Long Porcupine Island. The excitement of discovering new places often pushed the adventuresome to hike, bike, or sail to all corners of the island. When they got tired, they would find a spot on the rocks to munch on some egg salad sandwiches and chocolate chip cookies—just the thing for hungry explorers.

Photo courtesy of Mrs. Stockton Andrews

As THIS GROUP hiked the South Bubble trail around the mid-twentieth century, they could enjoy the natural beauty of the island's summits and valleys because of the foresight of many islanders, summer visitors and year-round residents alike.

One cottager, William Lawrence, summed up his years in Bar Harbor this way: "With each succeeding change we have been told that Mount Desert was spoiled: the old days had gone. But neither clothes, pearls, nor automobiles can steal away the beauty of the mountains, the glory of the sea and cliff and the bracing air. Compensations too, there have been, especially in the stimulating company. One of the richest contributions to my life has been the friendship gained at Bar Harbor and the companionship of able men."[11]

Photo courtesy of the William Otis Sawtelle Collections, Acadia National Park

Notes

The Island Settlers ~ pages 10–23

1. Prins, H. E. L. and B. McBride. *Asticou's Island Domain: Wabanaki Peoples at Mount Desert Island 1500–2000.* National Park Service: Department of the Interior, 2007.

2. *Bar Harbor Times*, August 8, 1934.

3. *Bar Harbor Times*, October 31, 1928.

Rusticators ~ pages 24–53

1. *Ellsworth American*, September 22, 1865.

2. Wilmerding, J. *The Artist's Mount Desert: American Painters on the Maine Coast.* Princeton, NJ: Princeton University Press, 1994, p. 195.

3. *The Independent*, September 24, 1868.

4. Lawrence, W. *Memories of a Happy Life.* Boston: Houghton Mifflin, 1926, p. 188.

5. *Ellsworth American*, October 9, 1863.

6. *Mount Desert Herald*, September 8, 1888.

7. *Ellsworth American*, July 13, 1863.

8. *Ellsworth American*, August 7, 1873.

9. *Ellsworth American*, August 23, 1877.

10. *Bar Island*, Paper in Jesup Memorial Library, no date.

11. *Ellsworth American*, August 8, 1872.

12. *Ellsworth American*, January 18, 1867.

13. *Mount Desert Herald*, September 21, 1882.

14. *Mount Desert Herald*, August 7, 1883.

15. *Bar Harbor Record*, May 22, 1895.

16. Haskins, D. *Diary of David Haskins*. Augusta, ME: Maine Historic Preservation Commission, 1879.

17. *Mount Desert Herald*, August 29, 1881.

The Cottage Era ~ pages 54–91

1. *Bar Harbor Record*, February 19, 1913.

2. Epp, R. H. "Garden Approaches to Acadia National Park," *Chebacco: The Magazine of Mount Desert Historical Society* (IV), 2004, pp. 54–63.

3. Amory, C. *The Last Resorts*. New York: Harper & Brothers, 1952.

4. *Mount Desert Herald*, August 17, 1884.

5. Smithsonian Institution Archives, Accession 96-153, image # SIA2008-2966 (old # 2.35).

6. Smithsonian Institution Archives, Accession 96-153, image # SIA2008-2967 (old # 4.153).

7. Jones, I. H. "The Gardens at Blair Eyrie," *House and Garden*, 1905, p. 173.

8. Metropolitan Museum of Art. Timeline of Art History: *Frog Fountain* [cited 2008 May 11]; available at www.metmuseum.org/toah/hd/abrc/ho_06.967.htm.

Refined Amusements ~ pages 92–113

1. Fahlman, E. "Wilson Eyre," *Biographical Dictionary of Architects in Maine*, III (12), 1986.

2. Lawrence, W. *Memories of a Happy Life*. Boston: Houghton Mifflin, 1926, p. 188.

3. *Bar Harbor Times*, September 18, 1912.

4. Peabody, M. L. "Old Bar Harbor Days," *Down East* magazine, 1965, pp. 34–76.

5. Smithsonian Institution Archives, Accession 96-153, image # SIA2008-2968 (old # 4.122).

6. *Bar Harbor Times*, July 17, 1912.

7. *Mount Desert Herald*, August 15, 1882.

8. Manion, L. N. "A Playground Contested: Bar Harbor Natives and Rusticators, 1875–1925," *The History Journal* (IV), Mount Desert Island Historical Society, 2001–2002, pp. 19–29.

New Occupations ~ pages 114–135

1. Cole, N. "Personal Glimpses of Bar Harbor's Lush Era," *Down East* magazine, pp. 42–92.

2. Barrett, R. *Good Old Summer Days: Newport, Narragansett Pier, Saratoga, Long Branch, Bar Harbor*. New York: D. Appleton-Century Co., 1941.

3. *Mount Desert Herald*, 1882.

4. Peabody, M. L. "Old Bar Harbor Days," *Down East* magazine, 1965, pp. 34–76.

5. Bunting, W. *A Day's Work: A Sampler of Historic Maine Photographs 1860–1920*, Vol. II. Gardiner, ME: Tilbury House, 2000.

6. *Bar Harbor Record*, August 17, 1893.

7. Salisbury, C. F. *Working as a Caretaker and Superintendent for the Satterlee, Ingalls, and Milliken Families*. Interviewed by Pamela Dean, February 3, 1981. Orono, ME: Maine Folklife Center, University of Maine.

8. RootsWeb's WorldConnect Project. *Blue Hill, Maine Founding Families*. Available at http://wc.rootsweb.ancestry.com/cgi-bin/igm.cgi?db=bluehillme.

9. Allen, E. A. *Recollections of Elizabeth Akers Allen*. Edited by B. H. Jesup Memorial Library. Bar Harbor, ME: Jesup Memorial Library, no date.

10. Bacon, P. Grant. *Bar Harbor Seventy Years Ago*, 1950.

11. Bar Harbor Fire Department. *Bar Harbor Fire Department, 100 Years of History, 1881–1981*. 1981.

Local Pastimes ~ pages 136–145

1. Allen, E. A. *Recollections of Elizabeth Akers Allen*. Edited by B. H. Jesup Memorial Library. Bar Harbor, ME: Jesup Memorial Library, N.D.

2. *Bar Harbor Times*, 1922.

3. *Mount Desert Herald*, 1883.

4. Cousins, A. *Working for the Potter Palmer Family and for Other Summer People as a Maid in the 1930s and '40s*. Interviewed by Pamela Dean, July 19, 1983. Orono, ME: Maine Folklife Center, University of Maine.

5. *Bar Harbor Times*, June 25, 1913.

6. Hill, R. A. *Discovering Old Bar Harbor and Acadia National Park: An Unconventional History and Guide.*
   Camden, ME: Down East Books, 1996.

Changing Times ~ pages 146–171

1. de Costa, B. F., *Rambles on Mount Desert.* New York: A. D. F. Randolph & Co., 1871.

2. Olmsted Center for Landscape Preservation. *Phase 2: Database Structure and Duplication of Historical Documents for the Historic Hiking Trail System, Acadia National Park.* National Park Service, 1996.

3. *Bar Harbor Life*, 1918.

4. Hill, R. A. *Discovering Old Bar Harbor and Acadia National Park: An Unconventional History and Guide.*
   Camden, ME: Down East Books, 1996.

5. Robshaw, L. *Recollections of the CCC Camps.* Interviewed by James Moreira, October 13, 2000. Orono, ME:
   Maine Folklife Center, University of Maine.

6. Pfaff, D. W. *Joseph Pulitzer II and the Post-Dispatch: A Newspaperman's Life.* University Park, PA:
   Pennsylvania State University Press, 1991.

7. *Bar Harbor Times*, July 7, 1949.

8. *Bar Harbor Life*, 1916.

9. Collier, Sargent F. *Green Grows Bar Harbor.* Privately published by Sargent F. Collier, 1964.

10. Roberts, A. R. *Mr. Rockefeller's Roads: The Untold Story of Acadia's Carriage Roads and Their Creator.*
    Camden, ME: Down East Books, 1990.

11. Lawrence, W. *Memories of a Happy Life.* Boston: Houghton Mifflin, 1926.

Acknowledgments

Without the help of many people, this book would not have contained as many photographs and interesting details for readers to enjoy. Earle G. Shettleworth Jr., the director of the Maine Historic Preservation Commission (MHPC), spent countless hours poring over more than 1,000 photographs to select and position the 255 that would tell the story of Bar Harbor's century, and he also edited each caption. Sargent M. Collier not only helped with the research and tracking down details, but he also contributed the captions for eight images (the top photo on pages 166 and 168, bottom photo on pages 152 and 160, and both photos on pages 167 and 170). Several of the 1940s photographs were taken by his grandfather, Sargent F. Collins. Debbie Dyer, the energetic and knowledgeable director of the Bar Harbor Historical Society, provided generous assistance in locating photographs from that organization's invaluable collection. For help with the caption about the racing yachts photo on page 169, we turned to Sturgis Haskins, who contributed his elegant writing style.

We are indebted to Christine Norris and Elizabeth Trautman of the MHPC staff for their support of this project. We called upon a few experts to write all or parts of specific captions, including Sturgis Haskins, Arlene Palmer Schwind, and Elizabeth Igleheart. Others contributed information for the captions, including Claire Lambert, Florence Ames, Nancy Howland, Library of Congress archivist Kevin Lavine, Alexander Phillips, Craig Colwell, John Clark, Bill Bunting, Ruth Soper, John McDade of Acadia National Park, Bunny McBride, Jeff Curtis, Jim McLeod, Mrs. Stockton Andrews, John Wall, Leslie Brewer, James Blanchard, Alison Salsbury, Steve Raab, and Charles Campos.

David Mishkin of Portland's Just Black & White photo lab worked his magic improving some of the old photographs. It was always a pleasure to visit with Raymond Stout, who gave generously of his time and willingly shared his photo collection with us. When I needed help on genealogical questions, Sheldon Goldthwait thoroughly answered them, and enjoyed a bit of sleuthing along the way. I appreciate the time that Elizabeth Gorer, John Goldthwait, James Blanchard, Corinne Graham, Dorothy Fillettaz, and Lois Frazier took to tell me and Sargent M. Collier about the old days. Many thanks to Boo and Dave Butler for their hospitality. I am indebted to several institutions for their collections, including Penn State University Libraries, the University of Maine at Orono, the Jackson Laboratory, and the Abbe Museum.

Our Down East Books editor, Karin Womer, not only provided guidance for this project, but also proved to have an abundance of patience.

Lastly, this book was truly a family effort, with content and editorial support provided by my husband, David Vandenbergh, and children, Christina and Alex.

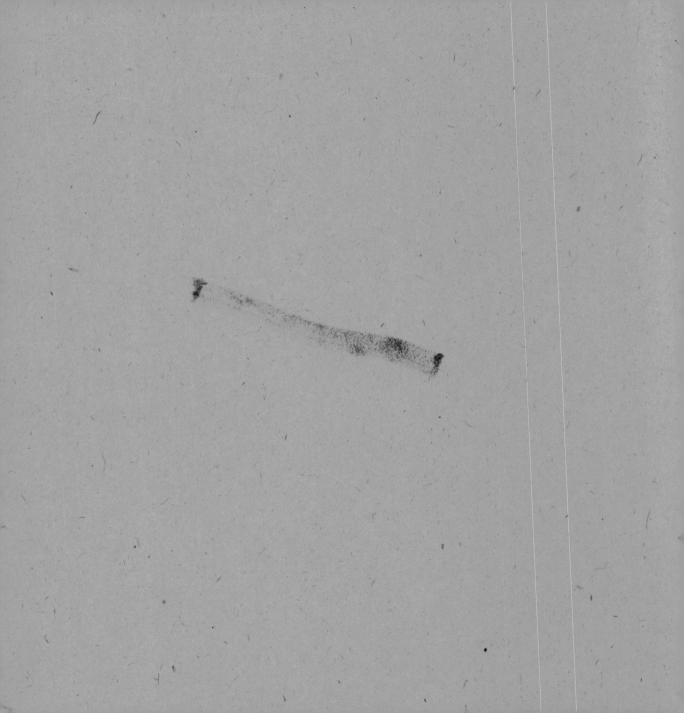

- The Colonies -

The Maryland Colony

Tamara L. Britton
ABDO Publishing Company

visit us at
www.abdopub.com

Published by ABDO Publishing Company, 4940 Viking Drive, Edina, Minnesota 55435.
Copyright © 2001 by Abdo Consulting Group, Inc. International copyrights reserved in all countries. No part of this book may be reproduced in any form without written permission from the publisher.

Printed in the United States.

Cover Photo Credit: North Wind Picture Archives
Interior Photo Credits: North Wind Picture Archives (pages 9, 11, 13, 15, 17, 18, 19, 21, 25, 27, 29),
    Corbis (pages 6, 23)

Contributing Editors: Bob Italia, Kate A. Furlong, and Christine Fournier
Book Design and Graphics: Neil Klinepier

Library of Congress Cataloging-in-Publication Data

Britton, Tamara L., 1963-
    The Maryland colony / Tamara L. Britton.
        p. cm. -- (The colonies)
    ISBN 1-57765-578-8
        1. Maryland--History--Colonial period, ca. 1600-1775--Juvenile literature. [1.
Maryland--History--Colonial period, ca. 1600-1775.] I. Title. II. Series.

F184 .B855 2001
975.2'02--dc21

                                                            2001022145

Contents

Maria's Land

Native Americans were Maryland's first settlers. They lived all around the Chesapeake Bay. Then, from 1498 to 1607, many Europeans explored Maryland.

In 1634, the Maryland Colony was formed. It was named Maryland in honor of England's Queen Henrietta Maria.

Early Maryland colonists were farmers. They grew tobacco and food crops. They lived in small, wooden houses.

Men worked the fields, ran the government, and served in the **militia** (muh-LISH-uh). Women kept house. Children helped their parents at home.

Later, England began taxing its American colonies. The colonists did not like this. They wanted independence from England. So they fought the **American Revolution**.

The colonies won the war. They created the United States of America. The Maryland Colony became the seventh state of the new nation.

The
Maryland
Colony

PA

NJ

Susquehanna River

SUSQUEHANNOCK

DELAWARE BAY

Baltimore ○

Anne Arundel
Town
(Annapolis) ○

Kent
Island ○

NANTICOKE

DE

POTOMAC

RIVER

PISCATAWAY

CHESAPEAKE BAY

VA

St. Mary's
City ○

Detail Area

The Thirteen
Colonies

NH

NY

MA
CT

RI

PA

MD

NJ

DE

VA

NC

SC

GA

ATLANTIC
OCEAN

Early History

Maryland is on the Atlantic Ocean. It has a coastal plain, plateaus, mountains, and valleys. Forests cover almost half of the state. Maryland has hot summers and mild winters.

Chesapeake Bay divides Maryland into two parts. The land east of the bay is called the Eastern Shore. The land west of the bay is called the Western Shore.

The Eastern Shore of Chesapeake Bay

Native Americans were Maryland's first settlers. About 6,000 Native Americans lived there. The Piscataway (pih-SCAT-uh-way), Nanticoke (NAN-tih-kohk), and Susquehannock (sus-kwuh-HAN-uk) were the three main groups.

The Piscataway lived on the Western Shore. The Nanticoke lived on the Eastern Shore. The Susquehannock lived north of Chesapeake Bay.

The Piscataway and Nanticoke were peaceful people. They spoke **Algonquian** (al-GON-kwee-an). Their villages were usually surrounded by **palisades** (PAL-uh-saydz). They lived in small houses covered with bark or reed mats. They fished and hunted for food.

The Susquehannock spoke Iroquoian (ear-oh-KWOY-an). They lived in large villages along the Susquehanna River. They planted corn, beans, and squash. And they fished in Chesapeake Bay.

Europeans called the Susquehannock aggressive and warlike. They often battled other Iroquois tribes for control of land.

The First Explorers

In 1498, John Cabot sailed along the Eastern Shore off present-day Worcester County, Maryland. Cabot was an Italian explorer. He was working for England. He wanted to find trading routes to Asia.

Giovanni da Verrazzano (gee-oh-VAH-nee dah ver-rah-ZAH-noh) sailed past the mouth of Chesapeake Bay in 1524. He was an Italian navigator who explored for France. In 1572, Spanish admiral Pedro Menéndez de Avilés (PAY-droh men-EN-dez day av-ih-LES) explored Chesapeake Bay.

In 1608, English captain John Smith explored the north end of Chesapeake Bay. Smith was a leader of the Virginia Colony.

William Claiborne of Virginia opened a trading post on Kent Island in 1631. Colonists grew crops, built a **palisade**, and opened a store. This was the first colonial settlement in the Maryland region.

George Calvert, the First Lord Baltimore, started the Maryland Colony. Calvert worked for England's government.

He was Catholic. But Anglican was the official religion of England. The English did not like Catholics.

Calvert wanted a colony where all religions were welcome and Catholics could live in peace. So in 1632, England's King Charles I granted the Maryland region to Calvert. But Calvert died before the king signed the **charter**. So King Charles granted the region to Calvert's son, Cecilius, the Second Lord Baltimore.

In 1633, Cecilius Calvert sent 200 colonists to Maryland. They crossed the Atlantic Ocean on two ships, the *Ark* and the *Dove*. The next year, the ships arrived on the Potomac River in Maryland.

George Calvert, First Lord Baltimore

Settlement

On March 25, 1634, the colonists left their ships and went ashore to Maryland. They bought a village from the Yaocomaco (yuh-KAHM-muh-ko) tribe. The village included houses, storage buildings, gardens, and canoes.

To keep the colonists safe, a **palisade** surrounded the village. There were seven cannons for protection against enemy attacks. The colonists named their village St. Mary's City. It was Maryland's first capital.

Many people wanted to settle in Maryland. There, they could start a new life. They could work their own farms and practice their religion in peace.

Men who brought five colonists to Maryland were granted 5,000 acres (2,023 ha) of land. After 1635, men who brought five colonists gained 1,000 acres (407 ha). Widows with children received the same grant as men.

The colonists built their communities near the water. Before they built roads, the colonists traveled on waterways, and on paths the Native Americans had made.

The local Native Americans were friendly. They taught the colonists how to survive in the new land. The colonists also traded with the Virginia Colony. There, they could buy cows, pigs, and wood.

Maryland colonists trade with the Yaocomaco in St. Mary's City.

Government

Maryland's **charter** made Cecilius Calvert the owner of Maryland. He was called the proprietor. Calvert could appoint judges, wage war, issue money, collect taxes, pardon offenders, make land grants, and create laws. But his laws could not go against England's laws.

In 1633, Calvert sent his brother, Leonard Calvert, to be Maryland's governor. In 1635, Leonard Calvert started an assembly of **freemen**. The assembly made laws. But Cecilius Calvert had to approve them.

Richard Ingle, a **Puritan**, arrived in Maryland in 1645. While Leonard Calvert was visiting the Virginia Colony, Ingle started a revolt. He took control of the colony.

Ingle demanded that the colonists swear loyalty to the new Puritan government. The Puritans believed biblical laws and church officials should rule the colonies. Those who refused to swear loyalty were punished.

In 1646, Calvert returned to Maryland with a small army. He regained control of the colony. Ingle returned to England.

In the 1650s, Maryland's government underwent many changes. England chose a commission to govern Maryland in 1652. Two years later, **Puritans** took control of Maryland. Then in 1657, England returned ownership of Maryland to Cecilius Calvert.

Maryland's colonists soon gained more control over their government. In 1658, the **freemen** of each county gained the right to elect four assembly members. The county **militias** met four times each year. And county courts received more power.

Cecilius Calvert

Life in the Colony

It was easier to settle in Maryland than in other colonies. Early Virginia colonists had already claimed the land and established a tobacco trade. And the Native Americans were peaceful. They helped the Maryland colonists survive. But there was still much to do.

Men ran the government. They attended government meetings and voted. They defended the colony by serving in the **militia**. At home, men built houses and barns. They also worked the fields and butchered animals.

Women were responsible for keeping house. They milked the cows. They made butter and cheese from the milk. They planted kitchen gardens. They grew peas, beans, corn, squash, and pumpkins.

Women also ground corn into flour, made clothes and soap, washed laundry, and raised the children. In poor families, women worked alongside men in the fields.

On Sundays, colonists rested and attended church. In 1649, Maryland's government passed the Toleration Act. It allowed the colonists to practice all religions without punishment. So Catholics, Protestants, Quakers, and Jews came to live there.

Maryland colonists making soap

Making a Living

Most early Maryland colonists were farmers. They grew grains, vegetables, and fruit trees. Tobacco also grew well in Maryland. Europeans bought a lot of Maryland's tobacco. It quickly became Maryland's most important crop.

To grow well, tobacco needed a lot of care. So the farmers needed many people to work their fields. At first, farmers used **indentured** servants. In exchange for passage from England, a person agreed to work for a farmer for seven years. Then the person was free.

Then in 1664, slavery became legal in the Maryland Colony. All slaves had to serve for life. They could not earn their freedom by working like indentured servants could.

Farmers began buying Africans to use as slaves. Slaves were property. Farmers did not pay slaves for their work. So slavery helped farmers and plantations make more money. Slavery was an important part of Maryland's **economy** until 1865. Then the Thirteenth **Amendment** made slavery illegal.

In the 1730s, colonists began using Maryland's waterways to make a living. Shipbuilding became an important industry. Colonists built successful mills on the rivers of the Western Shore. The city of Baltimore grew around one of these mills.

By the 1740s, the Maryland Colony had a strong **economy**. It produced wheat, corn, tobacco, and livestock. At first, the colonists sold these goods to European countries. Later, they established trade with other colonies.

Buying slaves at an auction

17

Food

The Native Americans taught the colonists how to plant gardens. They grew corn, beans, squash, potatoes, peas, and pumpkins. To grow these vegetables, they learned to use fish as a **fertilizer**.

The Native Americans also taught the colonists how to cook the vegetables in different ways. Colonists ate succotash, hominy, stew, cornbread, baked beans, and roasted corn. The colonists also enjoyed cabbage, carrots, and parsnips. Apple, pear, and peach trees provided delicious fresh fruits.

The colonists learned how to hunt, fish, and travel through Maryland's waterways. The Native Americans taught them how to make fishing nets and dugout canoes. The colonists hunted deer and bear. They preserved the meat with smoke and salt.

The colonists drank milk from their cows when it was available. They also made apple cider.

Corn

Hunters bringing home a bear

Clothing

Rich colonists bought fashionable clothing from England. Men wore silk coats and pants. Their white shirts had lace collars. And they wore leather shoes and beaver-pelt hats. Women wore silk, velvet, satin, or broadcloth dresses.

Common people did not have enough money to buy clothes from England. So women made clothing for their families out of wool and flax.

Some farmers grew flax. Flax plants have long, silklike fibers inside their stems. Colonists spun flax fibers into thread on a spinning wheel. Then they wove the thread into cloth. They made clothing from this cloth.

Colonists also made leather. To do this, men soaked animal hides in **lime** and water. This took the hair and tissue off the hides. Then they buried the hides in pits filled with tree bark. Tannic acid in the bark preserved the hides and colored them dark brown. Then they rubbed the hides with grease to make them waterproof. The colonists used the leather to make shoes, belts, hats, pouches, **bridles**, and other goods.

Colonists prepare hides to be tanned.

Homes

Maryland had plenty of trees. So the early colonists built wood-framed houses.

Colonists used hand tools to turn logs into posts and beams. They used these to build the frames. Then they covered the frames with clapboards. They made roofs from boards or wooden shingles. Brick or tamped earth served as a floor. The door was made of heavy boards.

The wood the colonists used to make clapboards was green and untreated. When the clapboards dried, they shrank. This left gaps between the clapboards, which let in cold air. So the colonists filled the gaps with clay. The chimney was made of sticks and clay, too.

The first colonial homes had a few small windows with wooden shutters. Some of the windows were glass. But glass was expensive. So some colonists used animal skins or oiled paper instead.

Many colonial homes had one large room. Some families also built a sleeping loft upstairs. Some houses had outbuildings and summer kitchens separate from the main house.

Later, when the colonists had more money, they built bigger homes. These homes were made of brick and often were two stories high. The first floor had two large rooms and a staircase. The bedrooms were on the second floor.

A two-story brick home from the colonial period

Children

When the colony began, there were many more men than women. Very few men could get married. So there were not many children in Maryland.

Also, most colonists were **indentured** servants. They weren't free to marry until they worked for seven years. By the time they could start a family, they were older. They could not have as many children as younger people. And many children died when they were just babies.

The children who survived had to help on the farm. Fathers taught their boys how to farm and hunt. Mothers taught their girls how to keep house.

There was not much time for play. When they had free time, children rolled hoops, played tag and marbles, swam, and fished.

Maryland colonists believed school was only for rich people. Wealthy farmers sent their sons to school. But their daughters learned to become homemakers.

Maryland's first school was King William's School. It started in 1696. The school prepared boys to attend college or to become Anglican ministers.

In 1723, a law required a school and a school board in each county. Soon, the government ordered that poor children be educated, too. But the schools were not built easily. Wealthy farmers did not like paying taxes for schools.

A young girl helps her mother with household chores.

Native Americans

When the colonists arrived in 1634, the Native Americans were friendly. They helped the colonists start a settlement. And they taught the colonists how to survive in the new land.

But the Native Americans did not do as well. Colonial settlements pushed the Native Americans from their homelands. But many did not want to leave.

At first, trading kept the colonists and the Susquehannock from fighting. But later they fought over land. By 1642, Maryland's governor had declared that the Susquehannock were enemies of the colony.

Attempts at peace failed. But by 1652, the Susquehannock and the colonists had stopped fighting. The Susquehannock signed a treaty that gave up their land.

Disease was another enemy of the Native Americans. They could not cure the diseases that the colonists brought from Europe. Many Native Americans died. Just 50 years after the colonists arrived, the Native Americans had almost disappeared from Maryland.

Native Americans constructing a house

The Road to Statehood

The Calvert family continued to play an important role in the Maryland Colony's history. In 1661, Charles Calvert became Maryland's governor. He was Cecilius Calvert's son. In 1675, Cecilius died. Charles became the Third Lord Baltimore and owner of the Maryland Colony.

But the colonists were unhappy with their government. They had to pay high taxes. And the best government jobs were often given to Catholics.

In 1689, Protestant John Coodes began a **rebellion**. He formed the Protestant Association. It took control of the government from Charles Calvert.

In 1691, England's Queen Mary II sent Lionel Copley to Maryland. He became Maryland's first royal governor. England ruled Maryland for the next 24 years. During this time, the capital moved from St. Mary's City to Anne Arundel Town. In 1695, it was renamed Annapolis.

The Calvert family regained control of Maryland in 1715. They ruled Maryland until the **American Revolution**.

Like other colonies, Maryland favored independence from England. Maryland colonists fought the **Stamp Act** of 1765. In 1774, they protested the **Boston Port Act**. Maryland approved its first state **constitution** on November 8, 1776.

Maryland troops fought throughout the **American Revolution**. Maryland's colonists built ships and cannons for the colonial forces. But little fighting took place in Maryland. The colonies won the war. Maryland approved the U.S. Constitution on April 28, 1788. It became the seventh state.

Today, manufacturing has replaced farming as Maryland's most important **economic** activity. Visitors to Maryland enjoy libraries, museums, state parks, and forests. They also visit Maryland's historic sites. There, they can learn more about Maryland's colonial past.

An American soldier loading a musket

TIMELINE

1498 - John Cabot explores Maryland

1524 - Giovanni da Verrazzano explores Chesapeake Bay

1572 - Pedro Menéndez de Avilés explores Chesapeake Bay

1608 - John Smith explores Chesapeake Bay

1631 - William Claiborne opens a trading post on Kent Island

1632 - King Charles I grants Maryland to George Calvert, the First Lord Baltimore

1633 - Leonard Calvert becomes Maryland's governor

1634 - English colonists arrive in Maryland

1635 - Leonard Calvert starts an assembly of freemen

1645 - Puritan Richard Ingle takes control of the colony

1646 - Leonard Calvert regains control of the colony

1649 - Toleration Act passes

1652 - The Susquehannock make peace with the colonists

1661 - Charles Calvert becomes Maryland's governor

1664 - Slavery becomes legal in the Maryland Colony

1675 - Cecilius Calvert dies; Charles Calvert becomes the Third Lord Baltimore and owner of the Maryland Colony

1689 - Coodes's rebellion

1691 - Lionel Copley becomes Maryland's first royal governor

1715 - The Calvert family regains control of Maryland

1776 - Maryland approves its first state constitution

1788 - Maryland becomes the seventh state

Glossary

Algonquian - a family of Native American languages spoken from Labrador, Canada, to the Carolinas and westward into the Great Plains.

Amendment - a change to the U.S. Constitution.

American Revolution - 1775-1783. A war for independence between England and its North American colonies. The colonists won and created the United States of America.

Boston Port Act - an English law that stopped Boston's sea trade until payment was received for tea destroyed during the Boston Tea Party.

bridle - the part of a horse's harness that fits over its head.

charter - a written contract that states a colony's boundaries and form of government.

constitution - the laws that govern a state or country.

economy - the way a colony uses its money, goods, and natural resources.

fertilizer - something that, when added to soil, helps plants grow.

freeman - a man free from bondage or slavery. A freeman often owned land and had the right to vote for assembly members.

indenture - a contract that binds a person to work for another person for a stated time period.

lime - a white substance that comes from limestone, shells, or bone.

militia - citizens trained for war and emergencies.

palisade - a fence of strong stakes placed closely together and set firmly into the ground.

Puritans - a group of people who thought the Church of England needed some changes, but wanted to stay in it.

rebellion - an armed attack on a government.

Stamp Act - a tax of all colonial commercial and legal papers, newspapers, pamphlets, cards, almanacs, and dice by the English.

Web Sites

Maryland in the Colonial Era
http://www.clis.umd.edu/~mddlmddl/791/communities/html/stmarys1.html#orig
This University of Maryland Web site covers Maryland's colonial period.

All About Maryland
http://www.state.md.us/
The state of Maryland's official Web site has historical information.

These sites are subject to change. Go to your favorite search engine and type in Maryland Colony for more sites.

Index